The Twelve Tribes

The Twelve Tribes

Andrew A Bonar

REFORMATION PRESS

© **2025 by Reformation Press**
11 Churchill Drive, Stornoway
Isle of Lewis, Scotland HS1 2NP

www.reformationpress.co.uk

Edited by Dr Robert J Dickie
Cover photograph: *iStock*/Gargolas
Cover design: Intermedia Services (Stornoway) Ltd

British Library Cataloguing-in-Publication Data
A catalogue record for this book is available from
the British Library

ISBN 978-1-872556-64-2

Contents

Preface

THE names given to Jacob's twelve sons are highly significant. They accurately convey information about the personal characters and the subsequent histories of these men, and the appropriateness of the names can also be clearly seen in the tribes that descended from them.

This book brings together a series of articles by Dr Andrew Bonar, a Scottish minister whose scholarship and devotion have left a lasting mark upon the Christian Church. His accounts appeared as a series of twelve articles in *The Scattered Nation*, a British periodical for converted Jews. As a mark of the respect commanded by Bonar, his essay on Reuben featured as the first article of the new magazine when it appeared in 1866.

Dr Andrew Bonar was not only a faithful minister of the Gospel but also a gifted author. A master of Hebrew and Greek, Bonar's ability to uncover subtle shades of meaning in the biblical text was extraordinary, surpassing that of many commentators. This may be often seen when he provides his own literal translations of the text. The articles on the twelve tribes are now presented for the first time in book form, and readers will discover Dr Bonar's characteristic insight and depth, coupled with his passion for outreach to the Jews. These studies comprise eminently readable devotional and practical essays, offering guidance and encouragement to all who seek to grow in their understanding of God's Word and his dealings with his people.

In preparing *The Twelve Tribes* for publication, Reformation Press is indebted to Albert J Hembd, Hebrew scholar, of Alvin, Texas, not only for supplying English transliterations of Hebrew words (using the system of Brill Academic Publishers), but also for supplying references to works by rabbinic writers, the first-century writer Onkelos, the German theologian Ernst Wilhelm Hengstenberg, and the biblical commentaries of Carl Friedrich Keil and Franz Delitzsch.

The text has been lightly edited, primarily to conform to present-day spelling and punctuation conventions. For the convenience of the reader, Scripture references from the King James Version [KJV] have been supplied. The authorship of footnote material is attributed in square brackets.

It is the prayer of the publisher that *The Twelve Tribes* may be a blessing to all who read it.

Dr Robert J Dickie

Introduction

IN the review we hope to be able to take of the twelve tribes, our object is not so much to inquire into their history as to trace the descent of each, and mark how each got its complexion from its forefather.

It is very remarkable that, for the most part, each tribe is spoken of—both in Jacob's prediction and in Moses' blessing—in terms that bear reference to the patriarch who founded it, and to circumstances connected with his personal history. As the sin of Adam spread its dark shadow over all his race, so in some degree the special acts of the twelve patriarchs affected all generations of their descendants. Mysterious truth—but truth that cannot be gainsaid!

Andrew A Bonar

1 Reuben

WE begin with Jacob's firstborn, Reuben. In Genesis 29:32 we have the record of his birth: 'And Leah conceived, and bare a son, and she called his name Reuben: for she said, Surely the LORD hath looked upon my affliction; now therefore my husband will love me.'

It was with something like proud exultation over Rachel that Leah exclaimed רְאוּ בֵן [Re'u ven],[1] 'Behold ye a son! Come and see what the Lord hath given me!'

She had been for a time suffering the consequences of the part she took in the deception practised upon Jacob by Laban. She had felt sorely the coolness of Jacob's love toward her, and had discerned also the apparent frown of Jehovah in her temporary barrenness. But now the sun has shone through the cloud, and very beautifully does she acknowledge the giver: 'Surely Jehovah hath looked upon my affliction.' She traces events to their true cause, the lovingkindness of 'the Father of lights' who sends every good gift. Family trials, as well as family mercies, are all from him. Secret wounds, heart-

---

[1] *Re'uven* is the Hebrew form of Reuben. Division of the name into two words (*Re'u* and *ven*) is a grammatically sound exposition of Reuben's name. This exposition of the name occurs in a collection of ancient rabbinical interpretations on Genesis known as *Bereshit Rabbah*—the Genesis *Rabbah*—a work only available in the original Hebrew in Bonar's day. [Hembd]

burnings, gloom, and smiles are not unnoticed, nor uncared for.

Then further, Leah expected much comfort from this gift. 'My husband will love me.' This is to be one result. This son shall be the cornerstone of the family building. 'See, a son!' This is another expected result, combined with the anticipation that of course she shall be looked upon with wistful envy by others. But alas! Like Eve with Cain, she was destined to be disappointed in the main subject of her exultation. As Eve fondly hoped that Cain, 'a man gotten from the Lord', was to be her comfort and joy, yet found him her bitterest sorrow, so did Leah, too, soon discover that this son of her womb was to be a sword in her bones, when in after years 'he defiled his father's bed' (Genesis 35:22).[2]

Sad indeed was the after history. Jacob felt it profoundly (Genesis 49:4), and was directed by the Holy Ghost to express God's abhorrence of the incestuous act by that prediction, 'Unstable as water, thou shalt not excel,' effervescing, or boiling over (פַּחַז) [pahaz] in insolent pride and uncontrollable desire, thou shalt pay the penalty.

Reuben, thou art my firstborn, my might, even the first fruit of my strength, pre-eminent in dignity, pre-eminent in power.[3] This thou art by natural right, yet because of thy sin the frown of Jehovah visits thee and thine: 'Thou shalt have no exaltation,' no distinction above thy brethren. The leadership of Israel is thus withdrawn from him, along with the

---

[2] 'And it came to pass, when Israel dwelt in that land, that Reuben went and lay with Bilhah his father's concubine: and Israel heard it.'
[3] KJV: 'Reuben, thou art my firstborn, my might, and the beginning of my strength, the excellency of dignity, and the excellency of power.' (Genesis 49:3).

birthright, as 1 Chronicles 5:1–2 particularly notes.[4] Neither he nor any of his tribe rose to commanding influence in Israel.

Sorrowful Leah! With thee, in thy crushed hopes, well could Eve have sympathized. If thou mournest over an adulterer of no common degree, she mourned over a murderer, a fratricide. Let no parent after this embark too much hope in such bulrush vessels. The gift may be prized, but must not be overvalued nor trusted in.

There is only one such vessel of which it is safe for us to boast—it is not Cain nor Reuben, but another son: 'the Son given to us' (Isaiah 9:6). Of him let us boast. Behold a Son indeed—God's Son! He disappoints no hopes, and to him must Eve repair in her bitter grief, and Leah with her blighted prospects, and Eli weeping his eyes blind over Hophni and Phinehas, and David groaning, till his kingdom hear it, over Absalom. 'Behold a Son!' (רְאוּ בֵן) [Re'u ven]. The true Reuben is God's Firstborn.

When Moses speaks of the tribe of Reuben (Deuteronomy 33:6), it is quite plain that the same Spirit is guiding his utterance. There is the same tone in his words: 'Let Reuben live! Let not Reuben die, and his men be few!'[5] This is all. No preeminence, even though his tribe would multiply as to numbers. His people are to be מְתִים [m^ethim—rendered as 'men' in that verse]—'mortals', not 'warriors' in any remarkable manner. It was at best the blessing that came on Ishmael, 'O that Ishmael might live before thee!' (Genesis 17:18). The sin of

---

[4] 'Now the sons of Reuben the firstborn of Israel, (for he was the firstborn; but, forasmuch as he defiled his father's bed, his birthright was given unto the sons of Joseph the son of Israel: and the genealogy is not to be reckoned after the birthright. For Judah prevailed above his brethren, and of him came the chief ruler; but the birthright was Joseph's).'
[5] KJV: 'Let Reuben live, and not die; and let not his men be few.'

this patriarch-father deserved death in every sense: extinction from Israel, as well as degradation. But pardon is granted: he is to 'live, and not die', though from him must pass away the birthright office of chief ruler, and all notable pre-eminence.

His history sounds through Israel's hosts in all generations: 'Flee youthful lusts!' (2 Timothy 2:22). 'Whoso committeth adultery ... lacketh understanding: he that doeth it destroyeth his own soul. A wound and dishonour shall he get; and his reproach shall not be wiped away' (Proverbs 6:32–33).

Still, Reuben was spared and pardoned; his name was on the high priest's breastplate, and a loaf stood for him on the golden table. And we find him in after days walking softly (may we not say?) in his appointed lot beyond Jordan. He did nobly in the seven years' war under Joshua for the possession of Canaan, when associated with Gad and the half tribe of Manasseh, and along with them received the meed [deserved share] of praise for brotherly help and faithfulness to his pledged word (Joshua 22:1–9). But this is the one only time that Reuben shines, and even then, he has no pre-eminence above Gad and Manasseh. So also when he contributes his share to the 120,000 valiant men who came to David 'with all manner of instruments of war' (1 Chronicles 12:37), there is no superiority claimed for him.

On the other hand, he shrinks back in the day of battle, when Barak and Deborah go forth (Judges 5:16). 'At the streams of Reuben there were great resolves of heart',[6] but what did they end in? In inactivity and unbrotherly withholding of help,

---

[6] KJV: 'Why abodest thou among the sheepfolds, to hear the bleatings of the flocks? For the divisions of Reuben there were great searchings of heart.' The Hebrew phrase means 'searchings of heart', as in the KJV, rather than Bonar's interpretation. [Hembd]

unlike his earlier days (Joshua 1:12–15), so that the prophet-ess upbraids him, and stigmatizes his unworthy attitude: 'Why abodest thou among the sheepfolds, to hear the bleating of the flocks?' rather than come on the battlefield and hear the trumpet and the clash of arms.

We read of the early captivity of this tribe (1 Chronicles 5:6).[7] It was among the first of the tribes carried into exile: proud Nineveh witnessed the spectacle of Beerah, Prince of Reuben, led along her streets in chains—the last prince of the tribe! His brethren, left behind in their land, were roused to effort, and under energetic chiefs recovered possession of the region 'from Aroer to Nebo' (1 Chronicles 5:7–8), and finding the pastures of Gilead unoccupied, quietly settled down upon them, enjoying a short season of tranquillity. But it was only the lamp shooting up 'a flickering flame' ere it sank away in its socket.

We said that once only did Reuben's light shine brilliantly. We may, however, add that in the days of Saul, they got some renown by a victory over the Hagarites (1 Chronicles 5:10).[8] In after times they sink out of view.

Once only was their territory signalized by any remarkable exploit. That one event was the Battle of Medeba (1 Chronicles 19:7–19). Within their boundaries also stood that mountain, never to be forgotten, viz., Nebo, with its summit, Pisgah, whence Moses viewed the land: a mountain of melancholy interest, a grave and a monument. And let us note that Heshbon and Elealeh, of which Isaiah says (Isaiah 16:9), 'I will water thee with my tears;' Jazer too, and Sibmah, over which

---

[7] 'Beerah his son, whom Tilgath-pilneser king of Assyria carried away captive: he was prince of the Reubenites.'

[8] 'And in the days of Saul they made war with the Hagarites, who fell by their hand: and they dwelt in their tents throughout all the east land of Gilead.'

Jeremiah plaintively laments, 'I will weep for thee with the weeping of Jazer' (Jeremiah 48:32), were in Reuben's land. Dibon also and Bajith were here, to the high places whereof they went up to weep.[9] Altogether we see the stamp and gloom of their forefather's sin ever reappearing in this tribe.

Nevertheless, in the latter day, Reuben's stains shall no more appear. In Ezekiel 48:6–7 we find his portion between Ephraim and Judah—a position of honour surely, indicating restoration from the fall in which his forefather involved him. 'Oh that the salvation of Israel were come out of Zion!' (Psalms 14:7 and 53:6).

Let Israel know that spiritual adultery, as a people, has been their ruin.[10] They left Jehovah, and when he came to his own, clothed in our humanity, when he stood on their hills and wept over them, they sternly rejected him. And never since that hour have they prospered. 'They shall not excel' is Israel's doom, as it was Reuben's, until they shall come in the latter day to wash away the stain of their enormous sin in the fountain opened for sin and uncleanness (Zechariah 13:1). Then shall they return to honour and excellency.

---

[9] Isaiah 15:2. 'He is gone up to Bajith, and to Dibon, the high places, to weep.'

[10] In 19th century usage, both in English and other languages, 'Israel' was a term used for the Jewish people, and it did not denote a political or geographic entity. [Editor]

2 Simeon

THE ear of God is at the world's tent door: he hears the cry of its sin. His ear is at the tent door of every family: he listens to what is said in love or hatred, in prayer or praise, by parent or by child. But the notice he takes of what he hears is not by words only; more frequently it is by deeds.

Leah knew this when she named her second son Simeon, which means 'hearing', significantly intimating that the Lord by the providence of this birth had taken notice of the unhappy disagreements of Jacob's family. 'Because the LORD hath heard that I was hated, he hath therefore given me this son also' (Genesis 29:33). The Lord had heard the upbraiding, the bitter word, the unkind remark—too frequent in Jacob's dwelling—from the lips of Rachel, and to rebuke her sent this gift of a son, not to her, but to her hated sister.

Earth is the Lord's larger family. 'Behold, all souls are mine' (Ezekiel 18:4). His providence is testifying among his own people that he hears the report of their deeds as well as their words, and soon they who speak 'often one to the other' shall discover that 'the LORD hearkened and heard' (Malachi 3:16), for his book of remembrance and his reward shall testify it to the full. Soon, too, all earth shall know it, for the due reward shall overtake each man and compel him to say, 'Ah, the Lord heard what I said and did! He has rendered to me according to my deeds.'

Because of the import and early associations of the name, it became common among the families of the other tribes, so that we have Simon Peter of the Sea of Galilee, old Simeon at Jerusalem, Simon of Cyrene; not to speak of others historically famous also.

At Simeon's birth it was what his parents spoke and did that was specially marked, but in after years it was Simeon's own evil report that came up into the ears of God. Simeon and Levi joined in unholy brotherhood to take vengeance, deceitfully, cruelly, and sacrilegiously on the men of Sychem.[11]

O Simeon, Jehovah is a God that heareth! In the days of Sodom, 'the cry of it came up to him', and 'the cry was very great', like the cry of the blood of Abel from the ground. But thy very name, Simeon, might have warned thee that thy deeds also must come to his ear.

Accordingly, his own father, with breaking heart, must utter Jehovah's sentence on him and his seed (Genesis 49:5–7).[12] 'Simeon and Levi are brethren, (yes, brethren in guilt and sin): their swords are weapons of wickedness. O my soul, come not thou into their counsel; with their assembly, mine honour, be not thou united, for they slew men in their fury, and houghed oxen in their wantonness; (they spared neither man nor

---

[11] Genesis 34:24–25. 'And unto Hamor and unto Shechem his son hearkened all that went out of the gate of his city; and every male was circumcised, all that went out of the gate of his city. And it came to pass on the third day, when they were sore, that two of the sons of Jacob, Simeon and Levi, Dinah's brethren, took each man his sword, and came upon the city boldly, and slew all the males.'
[12] KJV: 'Simeon and Levi are brethren; instruments of cruelty are in their habitations. O my soul, come not thou into their secret; unto their assembly, mine honour, be not thou united: for in their anger they slew a man, and in their selfwill they digged down a wall. Cursed be their anger, for it was fierce; and their wrath, for it was cruel: I will divide them in Jacob, and scatter them in Israel.'

beast).[13] Cursed be their anger, for it was fierce, and their fury, for it was cruel.'

This, therefore, says dying Jacob, is the sentence which I am called upon by the Lord to pronounce on them, as a protest against all deceit and violence. I utter it with reluctance, and yet without one misgiving as to its justice. 'I will divide them in Jacob, and scatter them in Israel.' Born at a time when his father's house was in a state of disunion, Simeon in after days, by his own cruel deeds, dissociated himself from the sympathy of his father and brethren, and now he hears that in the days to come, the tribe that is to descend from him shall ever bear the impress of this unhappy beginning. It shall be a scattered and divided tribe.

Now, was it so? We turn to the farewell blessing of Moses in Deuteronomy 33 to seek for Simeon and any word of favour to him there—but in vain. In their encampments at that period, his tribe used to pitch side by side with Reuben, as we find in Numbers 2:12: 'And those which pitch by him shall be the tribe of Simeon'—a host of 59,300 men. And yet Moses, whose eye had so often rested on these tents, has no blessing for him at the last. Did the infamous sin of 'Zimri, the son of Salu, a prince of a chief house among the Simeonites' (Numbers 25:14), slain in the act of his adultery by Phinehas, witness against the whole tribe, and bring to remembrance their first father's sin—as a recent wound often revives the smart of scars left long ago? At all events, Moses had no blessing to bestow on unhappy Simeon. Not that he had forgotten him, for in the commencement of Judah's blessing it seems as if he had the name of Simeon in his thoughts when he thus began:

---

[13] 'Houghed oxen' is an alternative translation given in the KJV margin. Most of the famed rabbinical commentators support 'uprooted a wall' as the correct reading. [Hembd]

'Hear, LORD, the voice' שמע קול [shama' qol—hear the voice].[14] Be to Judah in the better way what thou hast from the first been to Simeon in the way of rebuke.

Simeon's tribe was one of the foremost in going to battle against the Canaanites after Joshua's death. He nobly went up with Judah to war. 'Judah said unto his brother Simeon, Come up with me into my lot … and I likewise will go with thee into thy lot' (Judges 1:3). And they went together (verse 17), and at Zephath, or Hormah, won complete victory. Judah fulfilled his pledge of helping his brother, for this Hormah was allotted to Simeon by Joshua (Joshua 19:4). But then it turns out that this city and all the cities given to Simeon (such as Beersheba and Ziklag) were 'out of the inheritance of the children of Judah', so that Simeon is dispersed among the tribe of Judah, and has no separate portion assigned him as his own.

In this way, Jacob's prophetic words begin to be realized— and yet at the same time, in this very way, the dew of the blessing pronounced on Judah by Moses falls in part upon Simeon also. Indeed, at one juncture they seem to have out-stripped Judah in zeal. For, in the days of David's trial, Simeon furnished 7,100 mighty men of valour (1 Chronicles 12:25) to the Lord's cause, while Judah sent only 6,800.

But the after history of the tribe was destined to set forth a far fuller illustration of Jacob's words regarding their being divided and scattered. Simeon (as we have seen) never had any compact territory of his own, and probably it was because of this that he was ready to go forth beyond the borrowed pos-sessions yielded up to him by Judah. We find him, at any rate, setting out upon an expedition against Gedor, possessed by

---

[14] Deuteronomy 33:7. 'And this is the blessing of Judah: and he said, Hear, LORD, the voice of Judah, and bring him unto his people: let his hands be sufficient for him; and be thou an help to him from his enemies.'

the sons of Ham. This was in the days of King Hezekiah (1 Chronicles 4:39–41).[15] Perhaps the defeat of Sennacherib's mighty host may have revived the old faith and courage in the men of Israel, who could not but see that the Jehovah who fought for Joshua was Jehovah still. We find thirteen chiefs of Simeon leading a band of select warriors to this Gedor, where they come upon a people living in idolatry, quiet and secure (as quiet and secure as their father Simeon had found the men of Sychem, though in far other circumstances), upon whom they burst like a flood that sweeps all before it. It was an exploit that resembled the assault of the Danites on Laish,[16] this occurring in the far south of the land, as did that other in the far north, but both furnishing (may we not say?) a sample of the Lord's ways toward a thoughtless world. 'When they shall say, Peace and safety, then sudden destruction shall come upon them … and they shall not escape' (1 Thessalonians 5:3). It has been thus, and it shall be thus with all the earth when the Lord himself shall come.

---

[15] 'And they went to the entrance of Gedor, even unto the east side of the valley, to seek pasture for their flocks. And they found fat pasture and good, and the land was wide, and quiet, and peaceable; for they of Ham had dwelt there of old. And these written by name came in the days of Hezekiah king of Judah, and smote their tents, and the habitations that were found there, and destroyed them utterly unto this day, and dwelt in their rooms: because there was pasture there for their flocks.'

[16] Judges 18:26–29. 'And the children of Dan went their way: and when Micah saw that they were too strong for him, he turned and went back unto his house. And they took the things which Micah had made, and the priest which he had, and came unto Laish, unto a people that were at quiet and secure: and they smote them with the edge of the sword, and burnt the city with fire. And there was no deliverer, because it was far from Zidon, and they had no business with any man; and it was in the valley that lieth by Bethrehob. And they built a city, and dwelt therein. And they called the name of the city Dan, after the name of Dan their father, who was born unto Israel: howbeit the name of the city was Laish at the first.'

Here Simeon found pasture 'fat and good', but far from his proper lot, so that he is 'scattered and divided'. And then yet more. It is recorded in 1 Chronicles 4:42–43 that his valiant men turned their arms against a remnant of Amalekites who had settled among the hills of Seir. [17] That band of 500 warriors was led on by four redoubtable leaders, all sons of one man, Ishi, who had named his sons at their birth by names that spoke of the true ground of confidence, namely, Pelatiah, 'Jehovah delivers'; Neariah, 'Jehovah is the light'; Rephaiah, 'Jehovah is the healer' (or, 'Jehovah is the true Giant'); and Uzziel, 'God is my strength'. Their expedition was crowned with success, and Mount Seir became another settlement for the tribe of Simeon. Simeon is blessed, but he is 'scattered and divided', found in Judah, in Gedor and in the hills of Seir.

People of Israel, why are *you* scattered and divided at this hour? Why are you not a compact nation in your own land? Is it not because you have had fathers who, without any provocation (in this, far worse than Simeon and Levi at Sychem), 'slew men in their fury'? What men? The man Christ Jesus, the God-man, and his people.

> Why are Jacob's sons afflicted?
> Why is Israel still a slave?
> Has it not been long predicted
> that the Lord would Zion save?
>
> Why do heathen, proud oppressors,
> rule her sons with iron hand?
> Why are Gentiles now possessors
> of her long-neglected land?

---

[17] 'And some of them, even of the sons of Simeon, five hundred men, went to mount Seir, having for their captains Pelatiah, and Neariah, and Rephaiah, and Uzziel, the sons of Ishi. And they smote the rest of the Amalekites that were escaped, and dwelt there unto this day.'

Go and trace the sacred story,
there we read the awful cause:
they have slain the Lord of glory,
they have trampled on his laws.

3 Levi

THE Lord works for his own glory by raising 'the poor from the dust and the beggar from the dunghill, to set them among princes'. Out of strange materials, surely, did he rear up the house of Israel! And nothing might excite in us more amazement than his dealings with Levi, from whose loins he is pleased to cause a most noble line of priests and sanctuary ministers to descend. Sovereign grace! What may not thy love and wisdom bring to pass!

In the tribe of Levi, as in Reuben and Simeon, we trace in all after ages the taint of his first father's sin, and find that sin giving a peculiar complexion to his lot, while at the same time we trace no less distinctly throughout all after generations a reference to the origin of his name, which means 'joined', or in an abstract form, 'joining'.

1. At his birth, Leah thought that Jacob would be completely won over by this third son, presented to him as another arrow wherewith to fill his quiver. 'Now this time will my husband be joined unto me, because I have born him three sons' (Genesis 29:34). She knew the power of benefits, how a gift makes room for a man, pacifying anger and prospering a man's plans (Proverbs 17:8 and 18:16).[18] Probably her hope

---

[18] Proverbs 17:8. 'A gift is as a precious stone in the eyes of him that hath it. whithersoever it turneth, it prospereth.' Proverbs 18:16. 'A man's gift maketh room for him, and bringeth him before great men.'

was realized, for her next son gets the thankful name of 'Praise' (Judah), as if all were going on to her mind. From his birth, then, Levi was one whose province and mission seemed to be to join together parties that otherwise might have stood aloof and alone.

2. Next follows the history of his youth, and there he teaches how sin may join men together. In Jacob's prophetic utterance (Genesis 49:5), he appears as the close confederate of Simeon in cruelty and blood: 'Simeon and Levi are brethren.' What a union! 'O my soul, come not thou into their secret.' They combine: hand joins in hand, and the enterprise appears successful. But they who sin together must suffer together; they must be joined in punishment. And so the sentence comes forth on Levi, as on Simeon: 'I will divide him in Jacob, and scatter him in Israel.'

He drags this clanking chain on his foot in all succeeding time. He gets no portion or lot like his brethren, no compact territory, but is divided and scattered over the length and breadth of the land, getting forty-eight cities for his habitation, furnished by the other eleven tribes. He is to be found north, south, east, and west: in Judah, in Ephraim, in Asher, in Gad, in Reuben, scattered and divided because he joined Simeon in sin.

3. But there are other aspects of his history. The history of his descendants, who were joined to Moses at Sinai, teaches God's way of joining alienated men to himself. It was the day of the golden calf and its terrible scenes. The proclamation ran through the camp: 'Who is on the LORD's side? let him come unto me' (Exodus 32:26). None stirred a foot but the men of the tribe of Levi, and they joined Moses in executing the Lord's vengeance on the idolaters, for they girded on their swords, passed from gate to gate through the camp, slew all they met, even brothers and companions and neighbours—all in order

to win the blessing promised. For the clause of the proclamation was to this effect, 'Consecrate yourselves today to the LORD, every man upon his son, and upon his brother; that he may bestow upon you a blessing today' (Exodus 32:29). In this they honoured the holiness and justice of the Lord, dreadful as the action might appear, and this homage to Jehovah's justice and holiness was accepted at their hand.

Is it not ever thus? It is when a sinner is brought to sympathize with the Lord's views of sin, and with the Lord's justice in his wrath against it, that the Lord is reconciled to him. The sinner's acknowledgment of the cross, where the sword smote the man who was our Brother and the Almighty's Fellow, is equivalent to the action of Levi in drawing the sword against the sin around him.

4. Yet again, the history of Levi's descendants, who ministered before God in the sanctuary, teaches us yet more fully God's way of joining to himself alienated men, for the Levites stand there from age to age, handling the sacred vessels and engaging in the rites that exhibit the divine plan of reconciliation. It is they, and only they, who, as priests of Aaron's line, present the sacrifices—the blood, the fat, the incense, the drink offering—all, in short, that tells of man re-joined to God. He is Levi ('joining') in all his history. Day by day thus he in the atoning sacrifice set forth God's justice honoured; God's holy abhorrence of sin; God's flaming and consuming wrath against the sinner who goes on in his trespass, refusing to bring it to the altar and to the blood. Levi at Sinai, and Levi in the tabernacle and temple, is alike a witness for God's unbending holiness and immaculate justice, even while he receives the guilty in the appointed way.

It was on Levi as joined to the Lord, and as thereafter to be the tribe which should, in a manner, join others to the Lord, that Moses poured out his full and fervent blessing (Deuteronomy 33:8–11).[19] He begins in that blessing with the mention of the Urim and Thummim (Lights and Perfections—*i.e.,* complete light and complete perfection), but he nowhere describes what this Urim and Thummim mean. Many are the theories on the subject, but perhaps the simplest of all is that which understands it to be the law, which in the ark was written on tables of stone, but which within the folds of the breastplate was written on some other material, yet set forth the same truth, namely, that he who goes for us into God's presence, as priest and mediator, must have the law on his heart, must honour and magnify that law which is perfect, and which is all light and no darkness at all.

With allusion, then, to this typical priest, Moses sang, 'Let thy Urim and thy Thummim belong to the man of thy Holy One.' Let it be ever in charge of the appointed priest. The priest is called איש חסידך [*'ish hasidekh*] 'the man of thy Holy One' (like Psalm 80:17, איש ימינך [*'ish yaminekh*—the man of thy right hand]—that Holy One whom they tempted at Massah, along with the other tribes of Israel. Their share in that provocation is mentioned, that they might in no wise be elated because of this honour.

Let the breastplate which contains the law be ever in the charge of the priest who is at the head of thy tribe, and be thou ever zealous for that law, even as when at Sinai thou showedst

---

[19] 'And of Levi he said, Let thy Thummim and thy Urim be with thy holy one, whom thou didst prove at Massah, and with whom thou didst strive at the waters of Meribah; who said unto his father and to his mother, I have not seen him; neither did he acknowledge his brethren, nor knew his own children: for they have observed thy word, and kept thy covenant. They shall teach Jacob thy judgments, and Israel thy law: they shall put incense before thee, and whole burnt sacrifice upon thine altar. Bless, LORD, his substance, and accept the work of his hands: smite through the loins of them that rise against him, and of them that hate him, that they rise not again.'

thyself on the Lord's side, in spite of father, mother, brethren. This is the tribe who shall in all after ages have the high honour of teaching all Israel: 'They shall teach Jacob thy judgments, and Israel thy law: they shall put incense before thee, and whole burnt-offerings[20] upon thine altar.' (Deuteronomy 33:10). A blessed work, surely! showing men by type and symbol, as well as by clearer word, the way of acceptance with God—the way of acceptable worship—the way of daily service. And in so doing, his 'substance' is blessed, his 'works' are pleasing to God, and his 'foes' are powerless, smitten by the God whom Levi serves.

Now, this tribe being scattered all over the land in their forty-eight cities, with their enclosures (not 'castles', as translated in 1 Chronicles 6:54)[21] for cattle and flocks, walked everywhere as witnesses for God in the happy days of their early service, for Malachi (2:6) declares about Levi in those days, 'The law of truth was in his mouth, and iniquity was not found in his lips: he walked with me in peace and equity, and did turn many away from iniquity.' See those men of Levi at Hebron, teaching that lately arrived manslayer (Numbers 35:6), who has there found a city of refuge! See that Levite at Sychem, near Jacob's well, gathering round him a group of the men of Ephraim, to teach them the teachings which daily go on in the temple at Jerusalem! See them opening up the law to a company on the fragrant hills of Gilead beyond Jordan. See them at Ramoth Gilead or at Mahanaim or by the banks of Arnon, testifying by their very presence for God's justice, holiness, mercy, and lovingkindness. This is a joining tribe all over! He is Levi in his history, as well as in his birth.

---

[20] KJV: 'burnt sacrifice'.
[21] KJV: 'Now these are their dwelling places throughout their castles in their coasts.'

5. But Levi is rich in suggestive lessons, in almost every view you can take of him. We might teach from his case much about sin—*e.g.*, sin separating man and man, as seen in Jacob's family at the time of Levi's birth; sin separating man and God, as seen in the effects of his foul conspiracy against Shechem (Genesis 34:13–26); man, separated by sin, brought back to God through justice honoured. More particularly, we might weave a whole web of spiritual truth from the threads of Levi's history by using different stages of his existence to illustrate different doctrines. It stands thus:

(a) In the turning of his curse into a blessing, or, in other words, by making use of his scattered and divided condition as the very means of pervading Israel with the knowledge of Jehovah, we have an illustration of the Lord's way in redemption. While Simeon's curse ('divided and scattered') is left unalleviated, Levi's is used for great ends of good. This is altogether like the Lord, who in sovereignty passes by whom he will and shows favour where he will, but in both cases from reasons of highest holiness and wisdom, though hidden from us.

(b) In the history of Levi's youthful days, we see a full-length portrait of the natural man. It is forbidding and repulsive, exhibiting all the strength of original corruption. He was educated in Jacob's tents, under a godly father's care; was accustomed to stand at God's altar and see the sacrifice; often heard the story of his father's vision at Bethel; was kept as much as Joseph from the Canaanite idolatries; and yet, alas! the evil is unsubdued, and godly education is thrown away upon the man. Nay, fierce, cruel passions appear, and the young man rushes forth to gratify them. Under Jacob's roof the viper is nourished; under Jacob's shadow grows the all-blasting upas tree;[22] self-will, revenge, murderous hatred, are developed amid holy counsels and holy example. Levi, with his brother Simeon, even dares to use the sacrament of circumcision as a preparation for assault, urging the men of Shechem to use it, only in order to unfit them for defence.[23] It was a deed as foul as if we had persuaded an unarmed company to sit down at the Lord's table, and then came upon them with weapons of death as they were eating the bread and taking the wine. And what is all this but the unfolding of the natural heart, 'deceitful and desperately wicked'? Over such a one hangs the curse, the indignation, and wrath of an insulted God. 'I will divide them, I will scatter them!'

(c) Yet see how God can change the natural man and remove the curse. Go to the foot of Horeb on the day of the golden calf (Exodus 32:25–29),[24] and there you find how the Spirit of God had silently been penetrating Levi's families. Not only were

---

[22] In folklore, a tree which is alleged to poison its surroundings and is said to be lethal to people who merely approach it. [Editor]

[23] Genesis 34:24–25: 'And unto Hamor and unto Shechem his son hearkened all that went out of the gate of his city; and every male was circumcised, all that went out of the gate of his city. And it came to pass on the third day, when they were sore, that two of the sons of Jacob, Simeon and Levi, Dinah's brethren, took each man his sword, and came upon the city boldly, and slew all the males.'

[24] 'And when Moses saw that the people were naked; (for Aaron had made them naked unto their shame among their enemies:) then Moses stood in the gate of the camp, and said, Who is on the LORD's side? let him come unto me. And all the sons of Levi gathered themselves together unto him. And he said unto them, Thus saith the LORD God of Israel, Put every man his sword by his side, and go in and out from gate to gate throughout the camp, and slay every man his brother, and every man his companion, and every man his neighbour. And the children of Levi did according to the word of Moses: and there fell of the people that day about three thousand men. For Moses had said, Consecrate yourselves to day to the LORD, even every man upon his son, and upon his brother; that he may bestow upon you a blessing this day.'

Amram and Jochebed illustrious instances of grace and faith, with their three renowned children, Miriam, Aaron and Moses, but now behold: the tribe as a whole rises up on the Lord's side! How different from the days of Shechem! It is even as when the jailor was awakened by the Spirit, and his whole household with him. And thus Levi is consecrated to the Lord for ever, and becomes a tribe that does nothing but serve and minister for God.

(d) But again, in him we see the privileges of the new man. The Lawgiver himself (so just is it to deal bountifully with the forgiven) pronounces the ample blessing of Deuteronomy 33:8–11.[25] He gets guidance and guides others: God guides Levi, and Levi guides Israel. As it is still in the Church: God teaches sinners by a man taken from the same pit and miry clay, from the same curse and corruption. He has fellowship with God, approaching him with the incense, in prayer, praise, meditation, and multiform service. There is blessing on his substance, too, and he is accepted in his works (1 Corinthians 15:58):[26] victory is before him; he is more than conqueror.

(e) Once more, here are the new man's duties. Chosen, but not for any good in him beyond his brethren, he handles no more 'instruments of cruelty' (Genesis 49:5), but, on the contrary,

---

[25] 'And of Levi he said, Let thy Thummim and thy Urim be with thy holy one, whom thou didst prove at Massah, and with whom thou didst strive at the waters of Meribah; who said unto his father and to his mother, I have not seen him; neither did he acknowledge his brethren, nor knew his own children: for they have observed thy word, and kept thy covenant. They shall teach Jacob thy judgments, and Israel thy law: they shall put incense before thee, and whole burnt sacrifice upon thine altar. Bless, LORD, his substance, and accept the work of his hands: smite through the loins of them that rise against him, and of them that hate him, that they rise not again.'
[26] 'Therefore, my beloved brethren, be ye stedfast, unmoveable, always abounding in the work of the Lord, forasmuch as ye know that your labour is not in vain in the Lord.'

it is his part now to bear the vessels of the tabernacle (Numbers 3:6–8),[27] or, as it is expressed, 'to keep the instruments of the tabernacle of the congregation'. They enter into God's assembly, and each has his own department of work: none is idle, for gratitude constrains them, forgiving love presses them onward. But, as in the Church still, they do not all serve in the same manner. There are three families in Levi, of whom one (Gershon) carries the tent with its coverings and hangings; another (Kohath), the table, candlestick and altar; and the third (Merari), the boards, bars, pillars and sockets. So everyone serves, none envying the other, none complaining, none interfering, for God has appointed each one's sphere. They served in the desert, on its sands; they served in Zion; but at last they reached the gold-covered floor of Solomon's temple. Is not all this the history of the saints?

Besides all these teachings, Levi might furnish many other lessons. 'The LORD was his inheritance' is often repeated, telling all men where they will find enough. A true Levite's song was Psalm 16:5–6.[28]

Again, this was the tribe that furnished so many singers to the Lord's service: the Korahites, and other bands, with Heman, Ethan, Asaph, and the like. This tribe sent its representatives to David's help, armed for battle with twenty-two captains

---

[27] 'Bring the tribe of Levi near, and present them before Aaron the priest, that they may minister unto him. And they shall keep his charge, and the charge of the whole congregation before the tabernacle of the congregation, to do the service of the tabernacle. And they shall keep all the instruments of the tabernacle of the congregation, and the charge of the children of Israel, to do the service of the tabernacle.'

[28] 'The LORD is the portion of mine inheritance and of my cup: thou maintainest my lot. The lines are fallen unto me in pleasant places; yea, I have a goodly heritage.'

(1 Chronicles 12:26–28).[29] Of this tribe many were the thousands who gave up for the Lord houses and lands, glebes and manses[30] in the days of Jeroboam (2 Chronicles 11:14).[31] And there is something in reserve for them in the latter days, when the sons of Zadok, descendants of Phinehas (whose zeal won special promises for his seed), shall minister in that mysterious temple spoken of by Ezekiel the prophet (Ezekiel 44:15).[32]

How strange to find a name Leviathan ('the joined serpent') resembling Levi's. But very different is their history and work. While Levi, joined to God, and joining others, is a blessing in the earth, Leviathan (Isaiah 27:1), joined in his scales, is forming confederacy and gathering together earth's kings against the Lord and his Anointed. This crocodile of Egypt was the emblem of Antichrist, that enemy of God, who, with all his violence and power as 'king over the children of pride' (Job 41:34), seeks to disjoin men from their only Saviour. But the Lord's sword smites him (Isaiah 27:1),[33] while Levi, who

---

[29] 'Of the children of Levi four thousand and six hundred. And Jehoiada was the leader of the Aaronites, and with him were three thousand and seven hundred; and Zadok, a young man mighty of valour, and of his father's house twenty and two captains.'

[30] A glebe was the portion of land assigned to a parish minister in addition to his stipend. A manse remains the standard term for the house provided for a minister in Scotland. [Editor]

[31] 'For the Levites left their suburbs and their possession, and came to Judah and Jerusalem: for Jeroboam and his sons had cast them off from executing the priest's office unto the LORD.'

[32] 'But the priests the Levites, the sons of Zadok, that kept the charge of my sanctuary when the children of Israel went astray from me, they shall come near to me to minister unto me, and they shall stand before me to offer unto me the fat and the blood, saith the Lord GOD.'

[33] 'In that day the LORD with his sore and great and strong sword shall punish leviathan the piercing serpent, even leviathan that crooked serpent; and he shall slay the dragon that is in the sea.'

drew the sword for his Lord (Exodus 32:26–28),[34] receives the blessing, and along with his brethren takes root again, and reappears in holy beauties in the glory of the latter days (Isaiah 66:21).[35]

---

[34] 'Then Moses stood in the gate of the camp, and said, Who is on the LORD'S side? let him come unto me. And all the sons of Levi gathered themselves together unto him. And he said unto them, Thus saith the LORD God of Israel, Put every man his sword by his side, and go in and out from gate to gate throughout the camp, and slay every man his brother, and every man his companion, and every man his neighbour. And the children of Levi did according to the word of Moses: and there fell of the people that day about three thousand men.'

[35] Isaiah 66:18–21. 'For I know their works and their thoughts: it shall come, that I will gather all nations and tongues; and they shall come, and see my glory. And I will set a sign among them, and I will send those that escape of them unto the nations, to Tarshish, Pul, and Lud, that draw the bow, to Tubal, and Javan, to the isles afar off, that have not heard my fame, neither have seen my glory; and they shall declare my glory among the Gentiles. And they shall bring all your brethren for an offering unto the LORD out of all nations upon horses, and in chariots, and in litters, and upon mules, and upon swift beasts, to my holy mountain Jerusalem, saith the LORD, as the children of Israel bring an offering in a clean vessel into the house of the LORD. And I will also take of them for priests and for Levites, saith the LORD.'

4 Judah

THERE is nothing sweeter than a true song of praise. Every ear listens to it, every heart is moved by it, and God himself bends his heavens to hear. In Moses' record of a fallen world's history, the first time that 'praise' occurs is in Genesis 29:35.[36] It bursts forth from the house of Jacob and the lips of Leah, and may be said to accord well with that joyful boast of the Psalmist in after days, when he is led to sing that it is 'in the tabernacles of the righteous' you may expect to hear 'the voice of rejoicing and salvation' (Psalm 118:15).[37] It is in Jacob's tents that we first see one wearing 'the garment of praise'.

There had been a succession of blessings, like waves from the deep ocean, breaking at the feet of Leah, and when this fourth son was given, her exulting heart rose above its former self in gratitude. She takes up the harp: 'Now'—('this time' is the literal rendering, as if she had her eye on Adam's exclamation of delight in Genesis 2:23)[38]—'Now I will praise Jehovah!' And even as the happy mother holds the harp, she turns to her

---

[36] 'And she [Leah] conceived again, and bare a son: and she said, Now will I praise the LORD: therefore she called his name Judah; and left bearing.'

[37] 'The voice of rejoicing and salvation is in the tabernacles of the righteous: the right hand of the LORD doeth valiantly.'

[38] 'And Adam said, This is now bone of my bones, and flesh of my flesh: she shall be called Woman, because she was taken out of Man.'

newborn son and calls him Judah,[39] which may mean not simply 'praise', but 'one for whom Jehovah is praised'.[40] Indeed, the word is most expressive, involving as it often does the idea of acknowledging and confessing. Where the being and works, the name and excellences, the heart and hand of Jehovah, are spoken of, this is praise—and thus it is used (Psalm 147:12): 'Praise' (be a Judah to) 'the LORD, O Jerusalem.'[41] It is instructive to observe how the Lord, by repeated mercies, has melted Leah's heart, so that now, at any rate, if not before, her selfishness is drowned in praise. Nothing is so fitted to give a deadly blow to our selfishness at any time as real praise. Praise raises its note over buried self. Praise is sung when self is low and God high in our thoughts, and at such times, burdens roll off into Christ's sepulchre. It is at such times that heavenly work is done by men.

Such was Judah's beginning—like earth's foundations, laid amid the songs of the morning stars (Job 38:7).[42] And if Judah himself did not very remarkably call forth praise in after days, his posterity surely inherited this blessing—the sons of him over whom praise was offered became men of note. Jacob on

---

[39] Genesis 29:35: 'And she conceived again, and bare a son; and she said, Now will I praise the LORD: therefore she called his name Judah.'

[40] This is a quotation from *Commentary on the Old Testament* by Carl Friedrich Keil and Franz Delitzsch on Genesis 29:35. 'Judah, ... *i.e.*, praise, not merely the praised one, but the one for whom Jehovah is praised.' [Editor]

[41] The Hebrew words in Psalm 147:12 are not related to the name Judah, however. [Editor]

[42] Job 38:4–7. 'Where wast thou when I laid the foundations of the earth? declare, if thou hast understanding. Who hath laid the measures thereof, if thou knowest? or who hath stretched the line upon it? Whereupon are the foundations thereof fastened? or who laid the corner stone thereof; when the morning stars sang together, and all the sons of God shouted for joy?'

his deathbed foretells with reference to the name—and per- haps hinting at the sad feelings of his heart previously in speaking of Reuben, Simeon and Levi: 'Judah, thou art he whom thy brethren shall praise' (Genesis 49:8–12).[43] And not only thy mother's sons, but 'thy father's sons' also: the chil- dren of Rachel and Zilpah and Bilhah shall all 'bow down to thee'. And there shall be good reason why thou shouldest be thus honoured and praised, for 'Judah is a lion's whelp', one who shall early show that he is to command others. And did not this soon appear in Judah taking the lead in the desert march, and in going up foremost after Joshua's death to take possession? But 'the young lion' grew, and became indisputa- bly terrible to foes. Jacob sees him arrived at pre-eminence, anticipating the time when the historian of the past should write, 'Judah prevailed over his brethren, and of him came the chief ruler' (1 Chronicles 5:2), and so he continues his deline- ation of that career which was to entitle him to the name Judah.

'From the prey, my son, thou hast gone up!' Is not this the reign of David specially, when every nation round felt the tre- mendous power of Judah's king, when David prospered whithersoever he went, and when he dedicated of the 'spoils

---

[43] 'Judah, thou art he whom thy brethren shall praise: thy hand shall be in the neck of thine enemies; thy father's children shall bow down before thee. Judah is a lion's whelp: from the prey, my son, thou art gone up: he stooped down, he couched as a lion, and as an old lion; who shall rouse him up? The sceptre shall not depart from Judah, nor a lawgiver from between his feet, until Shiloh come; and unto him shall the gathering of the people be. Binding his foal unto the vine, and his ass's colt unto the choice vine; he washed his garments in wine, and his clothes in the blood of grapes: his eyes shall be red with wine, and his teeth white with milk.' In this verse, the Hebrew word for 'praise' is related to Judah's name. The word has the sense of 'confessing' the glory of Judah's tribe, in particular, because this is the tribe from which Messiah the Prince would come. [Hembd].

won in battles' an immense amount for the Lord's use? (1 Chronicles 26:27).[44]

'But see,' says Jacob again, 'he has lain down; he has couched like a lion! And like a lioness, who shall rouse him up?' A lioness is peculiarly fierce if her cubs be threatened. All this imagery sets before us the days when Solomon was King of Judah and Israel, quietly seated on his throne, honoured and feared by all the nations, none daring to do wrong to one of his happy subjects. It was then that Judah was at the height of his pre-eminence, the praise of all lands. After that period, nevertheless, he still held the high place assigned him, for did not all the noblest and best of the kings spring from Judah's soil? And the most renowned of the prophets? And all the sweet singers whose psalms and songs have been handed down to us?

Judah retained dominion too. The lion was still his emblem, and looking on through long centuries, Jacob was inspired to sing of this feature also in Judah's history: 'The sceptre shall not depart from Judah, nor the lawgiver (a ruler's staff) from between his feet, till Shiloh come, and the nations be gathered to him.'

Judah held his place as a kingdom till Messiah was born, growing up unnoticed 'as a tender plant', for Shiloh is no other than Messiah, the name signifying 'One who has peace', or rest, or security.[45] Messiah had rest and peace in himself, and came to give it to others: '*My* peace I *give* unto you' (John 14:27). And this name given to him here corresponds very much with Solomon, the man who 'has peace', and who makes others share it.

---

[44] 'Out of the spoils won in battles did they dedicate to maintain the house of the LORD.'

[45] The etymology of the word 'Shiloh' is uncertain. [Editor]

In all probability, it was in reference to this name of Messiah that the ark was so long kept at Shiloh, the town of Ephraim that bore the same signification. In due time, Messiah, long expected (but whose peace was not found at the town Shiloh, nor in the days of Solomon), did come, and ever since he came, the nations—not the tribes of Israel only—have been gathering round him, and giving willing obedience to him. From year to year, Shiloh has been gathering willing subjects, and shall never cease till he has gathered all nations as well as all Israel (Psalm 102:22).[46] There may be an allusion to the fact that for a time Jerusalem[47] was to be the resort of all true worshippers, but only till Shiloh should come (John 4:21–23).[48]

Oh Judah! What praise belongs to thee! What honour! Divine sovereignty has given thee the birthright pre-eminence. Well may thy brethren in all the earth join with thy 'father's sons' in almost envious gratulation [rejoicing]. Thou art he who wert honoured to give birth to Messiah, the King of kings, the Prince of Peace, the Saviour of sinners, the blessed and only Redeemer of the lost sons of men! All eternity shall remember thee.

---

[46] Psalm 102:19–22. 'For he hath looked down from the height of his sanctuary; from heaven did the LORD behold the earth; to hear the groaning of the prisoner; to loose those that are appointed to death; to declare the name of the LORD in Zion, and his praise in Jerusalem; when the people are gathered together, and the kingdoms, to serve the LORD.'

[47] The exact etymology of the city's name is uncertain. The suffix '-salem' is derived from the same root as shalom (peace) or Shiloh. [Editor]

[48] 'Jesus saith unto her, Woman, believe me, the hour cometh, when ye shall neither in this mountain, nor yet at Jerusalem, worship the Father. Ye worship ye know not what: we know what we worship: for salvation is of the Jews. But the hour cometh, and now is, when the true worshippers shall worship the Father in spirit and in truth: for the Father seeketh such to worship him.'

On account of all this honour, and because of all that his possessions in the land yielded him, Judah was yet further spoken of by Jacob as a tribe abounding in blessing. At this day, the inhabitants of Lebanon, when at vintage season they have stripped off the rich clusters of grapes and thrust them into the wine vats, tie to the vines the asses that have been helping them, letting them eat the leaves and branches as they please. In allusion to this very ancient custom, which spoke of vintage satisfactorily gathered in, and hinted at the gatherers having gone away to the wine vats, there to tread out the grapes, Jacob describes Judah's plenty of all good things: 'Binding his ass to the vine, and his ass's colt to the choice vine,' etc. (Genesis 49:11), enjoying all that might make the eye sparkle and the face flush with ruddy glow, while also they had their full share of the land 'flowing with milk'. Think of Eshcol and Hebron, with hills terraced to the top with vines. Think of plains and valleys covered with cattle and goats.

It would be easy to enlarge, but our limits forbid us to dwell on this feature of Judah's praise. We might add also that Shiloh the Prince of Peace, being a man of Judah as to his humanity, might be shown to embody in himself all the leading features of the tribe: praised—a man of might, the lion of the tribe, and yet the peaceful one, introducing the gathered people into an inheritance flowing with milk and honey, an inheritance better than Canaan.

In the blessing of Moses (Deuteronomy 33:7),[49] there is at first sight an apparently intentional ignoring of the name of Judah in reference to praise. It is of prayer we hear him speak: 'Hear, LORD, the voice of Judah!' But this also is part of Judah's pre-eminence. Yes, he is remarkable above others for prayer.

---

[49] 'And this is the blessing of Judah: and he said, Hear, LORD, the voice of Judah, and bring him unto his people: let his hands be sufficient for him; and be thou an help to him from his enemies.'

Was his first father so? Was not Judah that brother of Joseph who pleaded with his brethren (Genesis 37:26–27),[50] and then so pathetically [emotionally] interceded with Joseph himself? (Genesis 44:18–34). That voice touched Joseph's heart, and in after days the heart of Jehovah was touched by descendants of this same Judah, who were mighty in prayer. Such was Jabez; such was David; such was Solomon; such was Asa; and such was Hezekiah; not to mention more of the Lord's famous remembrancers. And in Judah, above all, stood the temple, to which the chief allusion may be made here, for it was 'the house of prayer', from which ascended supplication continually from the days of Solomon's prayer down to the days of the publican who cried, 'O God, be merciful to me a sinner!' No wonder Moses selected, by the Spirit's guidance, this feature of Judah's tribe.

We might further notice that it is Judah who has given name to the whole nation. They are Jews—that is, Judahites, because the tribe of Judah remained at Jerusalem when the ten tribes went into captivity and disappeared from view. And so again, O Judah, thy brethren and the nations praise thee!

But listen to one who loved thee truly—Paul who sat once at the feet of Gamaliel in Jerusalem. Listen to him reminding thee, 'He is not a Jew, which is one outwardly; but he is a Jew, which is one inwardly; whose praise is not of men, but of God' (Romans 2:28–29).[51] Come and join us in adoring Shiloh, greater than all the mighty kings, the true 'Lion of the tribe of

---

[50] 'And Judah said unto his brethren, What profit is it if we slay our brother, and conceal his blood? Come, and let us sell him to the Ishmeelites, and let not our hand be upon him; for he is our brother and our flesh. And his brethren were content.'
[51] 'For he is not a Jew, which is one outwardly; neither is that circumcision, which is outward in the flesh: but he is a Jew, which is one inwardly; and circumcision is that of the heart, in the spirit, and not in the letter; whose praise is not of men, but of God.'

Judah' (Revelation 5:5), and of David's line. He rests at the Father's right hand. Come and praise him, for he has shed the true glory over thy tribe. He is the true Judah, praised by his innumerable saved ones to all eternity, to whom he gives far better than the wine and milk of your famed Judaea.

O Judah, the Gentiles love thee for Shiloh's sake, for he was thy brother, while he was also thy Lord, David's son and David's Lord. We love thee, and all thy brethren, and we sing in our dwellings songs that breathe out our longings for the day when thou shalt again be a 'name and a praise among all people of the earth' (Zephaniah 3:20),[52] when 'Judah shall dwell for ever, and Jerusalem from generation to generation' (Joel 3:20).[53]

When the fair year
of your Deliverer comes,
and that long frost, which now benumbs
your hearts, shall thaw; when angels here
shall yet to man appear,
and familiarly confer
beneath the oak and juniper.

---

[52] 'At that time will I bring you again, even in the time that I gather you: for I will make you a name and a praise among all people of the earth, when I turn back your captivity before your eyes, saith the LORD.'

[53] Joel 3:17–20. 'So shall ye know that I am the LORD your God dwelling in Zion, my holy mountain: then shall Jerusalem be holy, and there shall no strangers pass through her any more. And it shall come to pass in that day, that the mountains shall drop down new wine, and the hills shall flow with milk, and all the rivers of Judah shall flow with waters, and a fountain shall come forth of the house of the LORD, and shall water the valley of Shittim. Egypt shall be a desolation, and Edom shall be a desolate wilderness, for the violence against the children of Judah, because they have shed innocent blood in their land. But Judah shall dwell for ever, and Jerusalem from generation to generation.'

When the bright Dove,
which now these many, many springs
hath kept above, shall with spread wings
descend, and living waters flow
to make dry dust and dead trees grow.

Oh, then, that I
might live, and see that olive tree
bearing her proper branches! which now lie
scattered each where,
and without root and sap decay,
cast of the husbandman away.

And sure it is not far;
for, as your first and foul decays
forerunning the bright Morning Star,
did sadly note his healing rays
would shine elsewhere, since you were blind,
and would be cross when God was kind;

So, by all signs,
our fulness, too, is now come in,
and the same sun, which here declines
and sets, will few hours hence begin
to rise on you again, and look
toward old Mamre and Eshcol's brook.

For surely he
who loved the world so as to give
his only Son to make it free—
whose Spirit, too, doth mourn and grieve
to see man lost—will, for old love,
from your dark hearts this veil remove.

Faith sojourned *first* on earth with *you*,
you were the dear and chosen flock;
the arm of God, glorious and true,
was first revealed to be *your* Rock.
You were the eldest child, and when
your stony hearts despised love,
the youngest, e'en the Gentiles, then
were cheered, your jealousy to move.

Thus, righteous Father, dost thou deal
with brutish men! Thy gifts go round,
by turns and timely, and so heal
the lost son by the newly found.

VAUGHAN

5 Dan

FROM time to time, during the long sojourn in Egypt, the blessings which Jacob pronounced on his deathbed would be spoken of, sung of at the brick kiln, and then on the parched soil of the desert, taught to their children and kept in memory as pledges of future good. Who can tell how often the bondmen encouraged each other, under the blows of the task-master, with the prophecy that Shiloh should yet arise, and Judah yet be the mighty lion?

But to teach them, when they had reached Canaan and its happy seats, not to rest as if they had found all that the soul could win, the patriarch Jacob, while in spirit in the midst of these future scenes, is heard breathing out his longing desire for more than his words have described. Pausing after his glowing delineation of Judah's lot and his stirring sketch of the prowess of Dan, he is led by the inspiring Spirit to exclaim (Genesis 49:18), 'I have waited for thy salvation, O Jehovah,' as if he had said, 'All that development of greatness and power in Israel is not enough. Oh, that the salvation of Israel were come!'

It was the first of a long succession of similar bursts of desire which used to find utterance when gleams of the glorious Saviour touched the chords of the believing heart. In the days of David, we hear the worshipper cry, 'My soul fainteth for thy salvation;' 'Mine eyes fail for thy salvation;' 'I have hoped for thy salvation, O LORD;' 'I have longed for thy salvation, O LORD' (Psalm 119:81, 123, 166, 174).

45

Isaiah cries, 'Say to Zion, Behold thy salvation cometh' (62:11), as if Zion were impatient with long expecting. Old Simeon exclaims at last, 'Mine eyes have seen thy salvation' (Luke 2:30), when at Christ's first coming he held 'the child born to us' in his arms. And the whole Church shall soon raise the joyous cry at his second coming: 'Lo, this is our God; we have waited for him, and he will save us' (Isaiah 25:9).

> I know that my Redeemer lives,
> he lives, and on the earth shall stand;
> and though to worms my flesh he gives,
> my dust lies numbered in his hand.
>
> In this reanimated clay
> I surely shall behold him near;
> shall see him in the latter day
> in all his majesty appear.
>
> I feel what then shall raise me up—
> the Eternal Spirit lives in me.
> This is my confidence of hope
> that God I face to face shall see.
>
> Mine own, and not another's eyes,
> the King shall in his beauty view.
> I shall from him receive the prize,
> the starry crown to victors due.
>
> C. WESLEY

But we have somewhat anticipated. Let us go farther back than to Jacob's blessing; let us go back to the birth-time of Dan, as recorded in Genesis 30:1–6.[54]

---

[54] 'And when Rachel saw that she bare Jacob no children, Rachel envied her sister; and said unto Jacob, Give me children, or else I die. And Jacob's anger was kindled against Rachel: and he said, Am I in

Man's heart has been called a microcosm, and a family is a miniature world. What we find in Jacob's house exhibits very correctly the state of the world at large. All things in Jacob's house seem out of order: envy, discontent, murmuring abound on one side; pride and the vauntings of rivalry prevail on the other. Rachel is against Leah, and Leah is against Rachel. Jacob cannot rectify the disorder, but at length Rachel hints that she has hit upon a plan which may adjust matters. She suggests that her handmaid Bilhah may have children by Jacob, and she will adopt her handmaid's children.

It is a plan such as only the unsatisfactory relations of polygamy would have admitted, but Rachel prayed over it—she says, 'God hath heard me' (verse 6)—and the Lord made use of it. A son was born to Bilhah accordingly, and while Rachel adopted the child and held him up as her own, she exclaimed, 'God hath judged me, and hath given me a son,' and so his name was called Dan: 'Judging'.

Now this term, 'judge' (which in Hebrew may be expressed by two verbs indiscriminately, דן [dan] or שפט [shaphat]), is one that includes much. It is, indeed, properly the expression for managing and ruling: putting in order things that were all confusion, or that threatened to cause distress. And so God is 'the widows' judge' (Psalm 68:5) when he manages her affairs for her in her helplessness, and he comes to 'judge the earth', as Gideon, Samson and Samuel judged and ruled Israel.

God's stead, who hath withheld from thee the fruit of the womb? And she said, Behold my maid Bilhah, go in unto her; and she shall bear upon my knees, that I may also have children by her. And she gave him Bilhah her handmaid to wife: and Jacob went in unto her. And Bilhah conceived, and bare Jacob a son. And Rachel said, God hath judged me, and hath also heard my voice, and hath given me a son: therefore called she his name Dan.

It was this rectifying and adjusting of affairs in Jacob's house that Rachel referred to when she uttered the exulting words, 'God hath judged me.' The storm of passion is quieted; the boasts and vaunts of rivals are stilled; order begins to reign in the tents of Israel, as well as in Rachel's distracted heart. In bitterness of soul and rash rebelliousness of feeling she had said to Jacob, 'Give me children, or else I die.' The Lord had heard her too, but he had also heard her bemoaning the sin and crying to him to overrule all. And the Lord *did* overrule, for 'he judged'. Even as he shall do in reply to the prayers of his elect, who cry day and night to him, 'Avenge me of mine adversary' (Luke 18:7). Men have, like Rachel, strange plans of their own for putting right a disordered world, but the Lord will overrule all.

In after days, Jacob foretold regarding Dan, with a reference to his name and the circumstance of his birth: 'Dan shall judge his people, as one of the tribes of Israel' (Genesis 49:16). He shall have his turn in judging Israel. And as he at his birth brought about a temporary cessation of strife and envy, so, when he shall have become a tribe, he shall be found performing a similar service. All this came to pass when Samson was raised up from this tribe at a critical period of the nation's history, to be to the whole land a deliverer and ruler. Not only did Samson for twenty years clear Israel's troubled sky, but he left his impress on the nation, who saw in him what might their God was able to communicate, so that truly one could chase a thousand. He caused the nations around also to know the same and to stand in awe.

But again, when he shall judge Israel, he shall do it in a peculiar manner: 'Dan shall be a serpent by the way, an adder in the path, that biteth the horse heels, so that the rider falleth backward.'[55]

In marching through the desert, Dan brought up the rear of the camp and may often have driven back the retreating foe. But the special allusion here is to Samson again, for like the serpent and the adder, see him suddenly, abruptly and by most startling strokes assailing the Philistines from time to time. Yet more, Jacob may refer to the Danites, in characteristic suddenness and force coming down upon the city Laish (Judges 18). These at any rate are outstanding facts regarding this tribe, related by the sacred historian in a way that may lead us to suppose that, on other occasions besides, Dan exhibited a similar peculiarity of temperament and character.

But further let us note, Dan in all these deeds was adjusting the balance, or 'judging', for even the affair of Laish was suggested by the tribe finding itself overcrowded, and by something of Rachel's desire to equal their rivals in prowess and possessions.

It may be because of the singularity of the description, 'a serpent—an adder', that there arose a whisper among the Jews and the early Christians that Antichrist should spring from the tribe of Dan—Antichrist: that serpent, that adder, and yet mighty ruler. Some of the Fathers thought their opinion confirmed by the fact that Dan set up the graven image of Micah (Judges 18:31),[56] and also by the omission of the name of Dan

---

[55] Genesis 49:17. '... so that his rider shall fall backward.'

[56] Judges 18:29–31. 'And they called the name of the city Dan, after the name of Dan their father, who was born unto Israel: howbeit the name of the city was Laish at the first. And the children of Dan set up the graven image: and Jonathan, the son of Gershom, the son of Manasseh, he and his sons were priests to the tribe of Dan until the day of the captivity of the land. And they set them up Micah's graven image, which he made, all the time that the house of God was in Shiloh.'

in Revelation 7. But for that omission, sufficient reasons of another kind can be given, and when we turn to Moses' blessing in Deuteronomy 33:22, there is no hint of evil having its peculiar source in Dan. Moses omits Simeon, but he mentions and blesses Dan: 'Dan is like a lion's whelp, that is wont to leap from Bashan.'[57] He is never to be like Judah—a full-grown lion and lioness; he is to be 'a young lion', making efforts at great deeds, and specially like the young lion in his daring leaps. It was in conformity with this trait in his character that he sent out his warriors from the south, where his lot seemed fixed, to the far north, leaping at once from the one end to the other end of the land. While adjusting affairs in his own tribe, he does unlooked-for things on the foe—coming on Laish all suddenly and irresistibly.

Shall not the Judge of the earth do the same? Shall he not come all suddenly, as the leap of a lion's whelp, upon an unthinking world, when they are saying, 'Peace and safety'?

There is a most interesting variety in the Lord's people. The Lord's tribes have each a characteristic of their own. Cephas is not Apollos, nor is either of them a Paul. There is variety in their gifts and graces in their lot, and in the results of their assigned work.

Often the Lord uses a man for some one great and important purpose, and then the man disappears from view. Micaiah announces Ahab's doom, Daniel's three companions pass unscathed through the furnace, Joseph of Arimathaea takes down the body of Jesus from the cross, and no more is heard of these men of God. So the tribe of Dan performs two great exploits—or rather, comes twice into bold prominence—and then disappears. In 1 Chronicles, while the other tribes have a place and mention in the catalogues of genealogy, Dan has

---

[57] 'And of Dan he said, Dan is a lion's whelp: he shall leap from Bashan.'

none at all. So also, Dan has one famous city, Joppa, but only this one that can be spoken of as renowned. This is the Lord's way, judging as he sees best, managing and ruling according to his will among the inhabitants of the earth.

One other fact about Dan. The architect of the Temple of Solomon was the son of a Tyrian, but his mother was of the tribe of Dan (2 Chronicles 2:14): 'a woman of the daughters of Dan', who had married a Gentile proselyte but was soon left a widow. How, then, is this woman said to be 'of the tribe of Naphtali' in 1 Kings 7:14? Because she, being born in that part of Dan which is in the north, and probably in the town called Dan, or Laish, had passed over to the adjoining tribe of Naphtali, and probably while residing there had met with a man of Tyre. In her widowhood, the Lord comforted her by giving her son singular talents and sending him to stand before kings— and, better still, to direct the building of the house of the Lord. Was not the Lord 'judging' the widow, managing her case kindly and well? And was he not teaching us that Gentiles were to come to the light of the Lord, and build his true temple along with Israel? Yes, Dan (true to his name and early history) suggests the right adjustment of the jealousy and envy, the boastings and the rivalry of Israel and the Gentiles. For as in purchasing the site for it, a Gentile, Ornan, had his part to act, so Jew and Gentile both are thus represented in building the Lord's house.

6 Naphtali

SOME theologians doubt whether or not the expression often used among us, 'wrestling with God in prayer', conveys a really scriptural idea. It seems to imply that the person who wrestles believes that something like unwillingness in God to give the request, or at least that his will needs to be wrought upon by great efforts of ours before he will consent to bestow the coveted gifts. Now, where the blessing is truly fitted to help and benefit us, there never is any unwillingness in God to give, and where it is not so, no wrestling of ours, no efforts, no crying and tears, shall ever bring God to consent to bestow it. On this account the expression needs to be explained, but it is a mistake to say that it is altogether unscriptural. In Colossians 2:1, Paul tells of his earnest prayers for the growth in grace of those of whom he speaks, and calls them αγων [agōn],[58] 'conflict', and in Colossians 4:12 Epaphras is represented as ἀγωνιζόμενος [agōnizomenos— labouring fervently], conflicting like a wrestler in prayer to God in behalf of the Colossians.

However, when we use it, let us clearly understand what we mean. We may use it surely since Paul did so. We use it not to

---

[58] It may be rendered more generally 'striving' or 'contesting', as in the public games, but Plato is in the habit of using the noun αγωνια [agōnia] specially for gymnastic exercise or wrestling. Either way, the violent exertion and effort is expressed. And see Colossians 1:29. [Bonar]

52

imply that God is unwilling, or that if we insist on it sufficiently, he will yield to us, even though he had purposed otherwise, but to express the truth that there are many blessings which he gives only after much waiting on him on our part. In short, importunity in prayer comes up to the true idea of wrestling in prayer, when it is such wrestling as that of Paul and Epaphras.

And if one asks, 'Why does the Lord in some cases wish us to employ importunity, and why does he not give the blessing till he has been urgently and repeatedly besought to do it?' the answer is obvious. Such waiting on the Lord, as is implied in importunity, is fitted to empty us of self, and the longer it is continued, may complete the discovery and deepen in us the conviction of our own worthlessness, and thus to fix our confidence altogether on the Lord's own grace. We really wrestle against our own fancied worthiness. This is a most humbling position, altogether unlike the other sort of wrestling (usually so called) which would convey the idea that the person who so prays has something of his own, has strength, has grace, has earnestness, which all may conduce to his being heard at last. Many have cherished this delusion, whereas it is only when we have wrestled against, and been emptied of, any such idea, left convinced of utter unworthiness, and brought to expect to be heard simply on account of the Lord's own gracious heart, that we prevail.

Jacob's case illustrates the whole matter (Genesis 32:25).[59] There you find the angel wrestling with Jacob, letting him for

---

[59] Genesis 32:24–28. 'And Jacob was left alone; and there wrestled a man with him until the breaking of the day. And when he saw that he prevailed not against him, he touched the hollow of his thigh; and the hollow of Jacobis thigh was out of joint, as he wrestled with him. And he said, Let me go, for the day breaketh. And he said, I will not let thee go, except thou bless me. And he said unto him, What is thy

a time put forth what strength he had till at last, in order to convince him of his real inherent powerlessness and worm-like worthlessness, he touches him and puts his thigh out of joint. Upon this, as we learn from Hosea 12:4,[60] Jacob, reduced to weakness, and probably agonizing in pain, seems to have fallen on the angel's neck, weeping and praying (for he had discovered his divine nature), and insisting that he should not go from him till he had blessed him. It was at this second stage that Jacob prevailed, for now the appeal was altogether to the grace and love of him with whom he had to do. It was only now that Jacob had become a truly scriptural wrestler, a wrestler like Paul and Epaphras in after times.

We are come to the history of Naphtali, whose name speaks of 'wrestling',[61] and this has led us to preface our inquiries by the above remarks. For there is some difference of opinion as to what Rachel's words signify in Genesis 30:7–8: 'Bilhah ... bare Jacob a second son. And Rachel said, With wrestlings of God[62] have I wrestled with my sister, and have prevailed: and she called his name Naphtali.'

---

name? And he said, Jacob. And he said, Thy name shall be called no more Jacob, but Israel: for as a prince hast thou power with God and with men, and hast prevailed.'

[60] Hosea 12:2–5. 'The Lord hath also a controversy with Judah, and will punish Jacob according to his ways; according to his doings will he recompense him. He took his brother by the heel in the womb, and by his strength he had power with God: yea, he had power over the angel, and prevailed: he wept, and made supplication unto him: he found him in Bethel, and there he spake with us; even the Lord God of hosts; the Lord is his memorial.'

[61] The name Naphtali comes from the Hebrew root פתל [pāthal], which means 'to twist, to become crooked'. It alludes to the twisting of wrestlers' limbs. [Hembd]

[62] KJV, marginal reading for 'great wrestlings' in Genesis 30:8. [Editor]

Hengstenberg and Delitzsch maintain her meaning to be that she had wrestled for mercy in prayer, to get God to deal with her as he had dealt with Leah,[63] and old Onkelos in the Targum[64] makes her say, 'The Lord has accepted my prayer when I did earnestly supplicate, that I might have a child like my sister.' It is against her sister she has directed her prayer, that her boasting over her might be silenced, and this she calls 'wrestling with God against her sister', for our version's 'great wrestlings' does not express the original. And so we may understand Naphtali's name as nearly equivalent to 'one won by prayer'.

Rachel, like the woman of Syrophenicia in after days, when apparently frowned upon, continued still to try the hidden depths of God's mercy. She was persevering and importunate in prayer, calling upon him on the ground of his infinite grace, while her sister Leah, satisfied with the past, made no such

---

[63] Ernst Wilhelm Hengstenberg, *Christology of the Old Testament, and a Commentary on the Messianic Predictions* (Edinburgh: T&T Clark, 1868), vol. I, p. 124. Delitzsch (in the Keil and Delitzsch commentary, vol. I, p. 288) remarks on Genesis 30:7: 'Naphtali, *i.e.*, my conflict, or my fought one, for "fightings of God, she said, have I fought with my sister, and also prevailed." נַפְתּוּלֵי אֱלֹהִים [*naptulê 'Ẹlohim*—fightings of God] are neither *luctationes quam maximæ* [Latin: the greatest possible struggles], nor "a conflict in the cause of God, because Rachel did not wish to leave the founding of the nation of God to Leah alone" (Knobel), but "fightings for God and his mercy" (Hengstenberg), or, what comes to the same thing, "wrestlings of prayer she had wrestled with Leah; in reality, however, with God himself, who seemed to have restricted his mercy to Leah alone." (Delitzsch).' [Editor]

[64] Onkelos was a Roman national who converted to Judaism before the end of the first century AD. It is believed that he wrote the *Targum Onkelos*, the primary Jewish Aramaic targum ('translation') of the Torah (the Pentateuch), in the early second century. The English translation of Onkelos reads: 'Then Rachel said, "The Lord has received my request by showing me favour when I prayed. I desired to have offspring like my sister; it was also given to me."' [Editor]

appeal to Jehovah. And thus it was that Rachel prevailed, and Naphtali was born, [65] the fruit of prayer—agonizing, wrestling, Epaphras-like prayer.

It is a mistake to insist that there is necessarily something like unbelief in such wrestling prayer, for it does not at all imply trust in our own efforts or distrust of God's good will. On the contrary, it is called forth by a fact regarding God's ways, which he has made known to us, and which the believing soul acquiesces in—namely, that he has delight in our continued prayers and would have us to be constant suitors at his gate, and that therefore he has arranged, as to some of his gifts, not to give them at a first or second asking, but only after we have continued perseveringly to ask. 'This kind goeth not out but by prayer and fasting' (Matthew 17:21). Jesus 'was all night in prayer to God' (Luke 6:12), and then obtained that quiverful of apostles. Elijah prays on and on till the seventh time ere the rain cloud appears. Rachel needed only to pray for Dan, but she must wrestle for Naphtali, and even then the full gain of her prayers did not appear. Ofttimes it is after we are in our graves that the result of our prayers comes full into view.

1. But we proceed. The gift won by prayer may be expected to be somewhat notable. What, then, have we to say of Naphtali's career as a tribe? We have dying Jacob's blessing on him, Genesis 49:21: 'Naphtali is a hind let loose: he giveth goodly

---

[65] Leah speaks of Jehovah, and Rachel of God (Elohim). Probably Rachel felt as if the Lord's treatment of her stood in the way of her claiming the blessing from him on any other ground than that he was able to do this thing, able as Elohim, even if not engaged to do it as Jehovah. [Bonar]. 'Elohim' is a general Hebrew term for God, that signifies his role as the Creator and emphasizes his majesty, power, and sovereignty. 'Jehovah' is the name of God that relates to the covenant relationship with his people: it is usually translated as Lord and written in capital letters [LORD] in English Bibles to denote its sacredness. [Editor]

words.' Others read it: 'Naphtali is a spreading terebinth; he putteth forth boughs of beauty.'

Whatever be determined as to the exact rendering of the Hebrew words in this blessing, it is clear that Jacob predicts that Naphtali is to be remarkable for some kind of beauty. Preferring the common rendering,[66] we find that the grace and beauty of the hind, as it bounds along 'with airy step and glorious eye', is Naphtali's emblem.

Now, this might well apply to the portion he inherited, for his lot fell in a region abounding in graceful and romantic scenery, where the 'hind let loose', the gazelle in its beauty, might be seen at every step, literally and figuratively. In his tribe are 'alluvial plains, long undulating ridges, and gracefully rounded hilltops, clothed with evergreen, oak, and terebinth; thickets, too, of aromatic shrubs, and lawns of verdant turf. There are glens, densely wooded, with streams murmuring among the rocks, and glaring [shining brightly] with oleander flowers, away down in shady beds. The air is filled with melody—the song of birds, and the music of the forest, as the wind sweeps its chords.' (Dr Porter).[67]

And then as to the next clause, 'he uttereth words of beauty,'[68] it has been suggested that they refer to the natural effect of such scenery in stirring up the soul to speak gracefully, if they do not express generally the fact that Naphtali's happy lot, by

---

[66] The Hebrew word signifies a doe, probably a gazelle. The term also features in the title of Psalm 22 ('To the chief Musician upon Aijeleth Shahar'), 'the hind of the morning'. [Hembd]

[67] Dr Josias Leslie Porter (1823–1889) was an Irish Presbyterian minister who led a mission to the Jews in Damascus. He published several books about the Middle East and contributed to Bible dictionaries. [Editor]

[68] KJV: 'He giveth goodly words.'

its rich scenery and verdurous landscapes, may be said to have been ever calling forth the eulogies of passers-by.

If, however, we go further, and inquire for the illustration of this blessing in the history and deeds of the tribe, there is nothing recorded bearing on this point except the memorable story of Barak and Deborah, the judge and the prophetess. Yet why should we not suppose an allusion to these illustrious leaders of the tribe, even as in the case of Dan the allusion was so pointedly to Samson? Barak goes forth with his ten thousand, like the hind let loose, and gains his high places (Psalm 18:33; Habakkuk 3:19),[69] while Deborah pours forth 'words of beauty' in her song. The hind was on its high places, as the prophetess sings (Judges 5:18),[70] and may be said ever after to have stood there, in view of Israel. Individual minds leave their impress on a generation, and on a region too. Barak and Deborah are the representatives of Naphtali. Nor should we forget that it was here Messiah first went forth, preaching the glad tidings, 'giving goodly words'. Some of his most 'gracious words' were spoken here, and six at least of his apostles seem to have been from this tribe.

2. But Rachel's gift won by prayer is celebrated by Moses also in Deuteronomy 33:23: 'O Naphtali, satisfied with favour, and full of the blessing of the LORD, possess thou the west and the south.'

The thousand captains with their 37,000 men, each carrying shield and spear, who joined persecuted David (1 Chronicles

---

[69] Psalm 18:33. 'He maketh my feet like hinds' feet, and setteth me upon my high places.' Habakkuk 3:19. 'The LORD God is my strength, and he will make my feet like hinds' feet, and he will make me to walk upon mine high places. To the chief singer on my stringed instruments.'
[70] 'Zebulun and Naphtali were a people that jeoparded their lives unto the death in the high places of the field.'

12:34),[71] attest the blessing which had rested on the population of their region. And then as to the region itself, some
understand the latter clause to mean that 'Naphtali shall possess a lot which should combine the advantages of the healthy
sea breeze with the grateful warmth of the south' (Keil).[72] But,
more definitely, we may remark that this tribe possessed at
once some of the most delightful valleys of Anti-Lebanon[73]
(where 'favour and fulness of blessing' rested beyond dis-
pute), and at the same time the fertile slopes which close in
the Sea of Galilee. On the south of his portion a part of this sea
lies, so that when Jesus walked on its shores, the prophet in
vision, and the evangelist in after days, exclaimed, 'The land
of Naphtali, the way of the sea! The people that sat in darkness
saw great light.' (Isaiah 9:1–2; Matthew 4:15–16).[74]

In the plain of Gennesaret, which Josephus calls a very para-
dise for beauty and delight, and where was concentrated all
that might set forth Naphtali as 'satisfied with favour, and full
of the blessing of the Lord', Messiah delighted to sound his
jubilee trumpet of deliverance, and utter his 'goodly words' of

---

[71] 'And of Naphtali a thousand captains, and with them with shield
and spear thirty and seven thousand.'
[72] Keil and Delitzsch, vol. I, pp. 510–1 (comments on Deuteronomy
33:23). [Editor]
[73] The Anti-Lebanon mountains extend northwards from the Golan
Heights, and form most of the border between Lebanon and Syria.
Mount Hermon (9232 feet) is the highest peak in the range. [Editor]
[74] Isaiah 9:1–2. 'Nevertheless the dimness shall not be such as was
in her vexation, when at the first he lightly afflicted the land of
Zebulun and the land of Naphtali, and afterward did more
grievously afflict her by the way of the sea, beyond Jordan, in Galilee
of the nations. The people that walked in darkness have seen a great
light: they that dwell in the land of the shadow of death, upon them
hath the light shined.' Matthew 4:15–16. 'The land of Zabulon, and
the land of Nephthalim, by the way of the sea, beyond Jordan, Galilee
of the Gentiles; the people which sat in darkness saw great light; and
to them which sat in the region and shadow of death light is sprung
up.'

light and life. His parables were spoken there, and many of his most gracious words, such as that everlastingly memorable invitation: 'Come unto me, all ye that labour and are heavy laden, and I will give you rest.' Bethsaida and Capernaum were towns of Naphtali, in whose every street might be found some memorial of his mighty works or some echo of his gracious words.

Even at this time, the traveller climbs the range of hills in this tribe, called Mount Naphtali, and finds every height well wooded, and often fragrant with the myrtle and aromatic shrubs, with cornfields at their base. Or he turns aside to the site of the old city of refuge, Kedesh-Naphtali, now called Kedes, and finds its ruins beside a modern village on a knoll, which rises up from a green vale, with herbage-clad hills beyond, and rich olive groves close at hand.[75] These are relics of the favour and blessing which the Lord once caused to rest here, when this tribe was like 'the gazelle let loose' or 'the spreading terebinth'.

It was when Israel turned to idols that the scene changed, and this tribe was the very first carried captive to Assyria (2 Kings 15:29),[76] its inhabitants swept away to the far-off region where now the Nestorians are found keeping up traditions of the past.[77] Perhaps it is no stretch of fancy to say that just

---

[75] Identification of the biblical Kedesh-Naphtali has been the subject of archaeological and historical debate. It is difficult to find information on these ruins today. Bonar likely had information about Kedes from his journeys to Palestine. [Hembd]

[76] 'In the days of Pekah king of Israel came Tiglath-pileser king of Assyria, and took Ijon, and Abel-beth-maachah, and Janoah, and Kedesh, and Hazor, and Gilead, and Galilee, all the land of Naphtali, and carried them captive to Assyria.'

[77] The Nestorian Church is a branch of Syriac Christianity. Over the course of history, it has been known by several names, and is nowadays called 'The Holy Apostolic Catholic Assyrian Church of the

because this tribe was thus the first to suffer under the stroke of wrath, Messiah, when he came (in the wondrous love and grace that marked all his ways), selected their borders as the scene of his earliest public ministrations. Some of his first and sweetest calls rang through Naphtali's groves and glades, and were echoed by his mountains. But they 'received him not', and thus they confirmed their doom.

3. Such, then, was Naphtali. Such were the after-fruits of Rachel's wrestlings. It is no vain thing to take hold on God's name and plead importunately. The fruit of such wrestling prayer is both present and future blessing. Saints under the New Testament have learnt this secret, betaking themselves to such wrestlings of faith, when they would go forth 'satisfied with favour, and full of the blessing of the Lord', 'like hinds let loose, giving goodly words'.

One man of prayer, when sent for by his bitter persecutors in order to be conducted to a prison, calmly replied, 'I know not whither you are sending me, but my heart is as full of comfort as it can hold.' And another man of prayer, as he is about to close his eyes in death, cries aloud, 'I am full of the consolations of Christ!' All this they possess through Jesus Messiah, accepted and rested in as theirs.

We inherit more than Naphtali's portion when we welcome Messiah, whose goodly words were uttered so often in Naphtali's cities—Chorazin, Bethsaida and Capernaum. Nor, on the other hand, is it ever to be forgotten how these once-famous cities were brought low—'brought down to hell'. The Lord Jesus came to them with all his saving grace. He would have gathered them under his wing, and 'they would not'. What then? Rejecting Messiah, a blight passed over them—a

---

East'. Nestorius was the Archbishop of Constantinople from 428 until he was deposed for heresy by the Council of Ephesus in 431. [Editor]

withering blight—and soon were they dispossessed of their pleasant portion, and lost at once the temporal and the spiritual riches that were within their reach.

And has not all Israel lost the pleasant land by the same unbelief? Why are 'few men left' in your land, O Israel? Why are your 'cities without inhabitants'? (Isaiah 24:6; 6:11–12).[78] Your house is left unto you desolate, because you will not say, 'Blessed is he that has come in the name of the Lord,' for so Messiah has spoken (Matthew 23:39).[79]

---

[78] Isaiah 24:6. 'Therefore hath the curse devoured the earth, and they that dwell therein are desolate: therefore the inhabitants of the earth are burned, and few men left.' Isaiah 6:11–12. 'Then said I, Lord, how long? And he answered, Until the cities be wasted without inhabitant, and the houses without man, and the land be utterly desolate, and the LORD have removed men far away, and there be a great forsaking in the midst of the land.'
[79] Matthew 23:38–39. 'Behold, your house is left unto you desolate. For I say unto you, Ye shall not see me henceforth, till ye shall say, Blessed is he that cometh in the name of the Lord.'

7 Gad

WE have been taking up the history of the tribes in the order of their first father's birth. But it is curious to observe in what great variety of order their names are given in other places, as if the Lord would show impartial regard to each tribe, by putting one in the place of the other from time to time. We have the following varieties, twenty-one in all:

- the order of their birth (Genesis 29, 30, and 35)
- enumeration of them at Mamre (Genesis 35:23–26)
- enumeration of them on going down to Egypt (Genesis 46:8–19)
- enumeration of them in Jacob's blessing (Genesis 49)
- enumeration of them when the heads of tribes are named (Numbers 1:5–15)
- enumeration of them when the males above twenty years are named (Numbers 1:20–43)
- the order in which they pitched round the tabernacle (Numbers 2)
- the order in which the princes offered (Numbers 7)
- the order in which they marched (Numbers 10)
- the order in which spies from each tribe were selected (Numbers 13)
- the order in which they were numbered in the plains of Moab (Numbers 26)
- the order in which the princes who were to divide the land were appointed (Numbers 34)

- the order in which they stood on Ebal and Gerizim (Deuteronomy 27)
- the order in which they were blessed by Moses (Deuteronomy 33)
- the order in which the lot was cast for each (Joshua 13, 14)
- the order in which the lot fell for the Levitical cities out of each (Joshua 21:4–8)
- the order in which the names of these cities for each are given (Joshua 21:9–39)
- the order in which the same are given in the 1st Book of Chronicles (1 Chronicles 6:55–81)
- the order in which their future portion in the Lord is given (Ezekiel 48:2–28)
- the order in which the gates of the city that bear their names occur (Ezekiel 48:31–34)
- the order in which the twelve thousand sealed ones from each tribe are given (Revelation 7)

Sometimes reasons may be assigned for the special orders adopted; at other times we can see none. In the new division of the land in Ezekiel 48, Gad (the tribe we now come to speak of) is placed in the far south of Palestine, reaching to Kadesh-barnea. In Revelation 7:5, Gad stands third in order.

The birth of the father of this tribe is related in Genesis 30:9–11.[80] Leah seeing the success of her sister's plan, and feeling herself neglected, adopts that very plan, and by her handmaid Zilpah gives Jacob another son. Her words on hearing of the birth of this son, have been interpreted by some as simply meaning 'Good luck!'—an exclamation of delight and satisfaction. But the better interpretation, which both retains the

---

[80] 'When Leah saw that she had left bearing, she took Zilpah her maid, and gave her Jacob to wife. And Zilpah Leah's maid bare Jacob a son. And Leah said, A troop cometh: and she called his name Gad.'

Masoretic reading of the text, and accords with Jacob's reference to the name in 49:19, renders the words, 'A troop cometh.' This is the sense given in the margin of our version.[81] Leah probably intended to exult over her sister (verse 11). 'You must leave the field to me again, for see! here is "a troop coming to my help".' Thus understood, Gad's name tells of defeat repaired, of conquering when all seemed lost, of clouds breaking up and sunshine returning after rain.

How often in the scenes of everyday life may we hear Gad's name. A family is threatened with disaster; gloom overspreads every countenance; disease has assailed some beloved one and death is hovering over the dwelling. But the Lord sends relief, perhaps in the way of leading the family to adopt a remedy which some other has tried. It is blessed, and lo! 'A troop cometh': relief and recovery have come, and drive the enemy from the field. Or the family is poor, care and dismal forebodings harass them, ruin stalks on the threshold. But means of relief are suggested, and found successful: 'A troop cometh!' It may be in the shape of employment given, or money sent, or friends raised up. At any rate, the clouds are dispersed, and one says to another, 'Oh that men would praise the Lord for his goodness!'

Nor is it less often thus in the family of God. God's children have dreaded their subjection to indwelling sin, for corruption has lifted its head. But 'a troop cometh!' and the despairing believer sings, 'I thank God through Christ Jesus my Lord.' Or it may be a host of outward evils assail: 'tribulation, persecution, nakedness, distress, famine, sword'. But soon there is heard the cry, 'A troop cometh!'—Paul and all his fellow believers singing, 'I am persuaded that neither death, nor life, nor angels, nor principalities, nor powers, nor things present,

---

[81] The marginal note is: 'Gad: that is, A troop, or, company.' [Editor]

nor things to come, nor height, nor depth, nor any other cre-
ated thing, shall separate us from the love of God, which is in
Jesus Christ our Lord' (Romans 8:38–39). Yes, even when
death, the last enemy, assails, this shall be the issue. With
Leah's battle cry he shall drive him from the field.

But let us see what Jacob said of his son Gad in Genesis 49:19.
He blesses him thus: 'Gad, a troop shall overcome him: but he
shall overcome at the last.' This may be rendered, preserving
the alliteration of the original, and rendering very literally:
'The troop-tribe, a troop shall troop upon him; but he shall
troop upon the heel.' He shall be a tribe much engaged in con-
flicts, and fitted for such warfare, so that he shall be found
'trooping upon the heel', putting to flight and pursuing his foe.

As a tribe, his geographical situation exposed him to invasion
from many quarters, such as Moab, Ammon and the sons of
Ishmael, but for this warfare he shall be fitted. Accordingly,
we find not only Bani, a Gadite, one of David's mighty men (2
Samuel 23:36) and even Levites residing in it, 'mighty men of
valour' (1 Chronicles 26:31), but a great band, who are
described as 'men of might, men of the host fit for the battle,
that could handle shield and buckler, whose faces were like
the faces of lions' (compare Deuteronomy 33:20),[82] and who
'were as the roes upon the mountains in speed' (1 Chronicles
12:8).[83] And then, along with Reubenites and Manassehites,
they of Gad came, 'with all manner of instruments of war for
the battle', forming a band of 120,000 men (1 Chronicles
12:37).[84]

---

[82] 'And of Gad he said, Blessed be he that enlargeth Gad: he dwelleth
as a lion, and teareth the arm with the crown of the head.'
[83] 'As swift as the roes upon the mountains.'
[84] 'And on the other side of Jordan, of the Reubenites, and the
Gadites, and of the half tribe of Manasseh, with all manner of instruments of war for the battle, an hundred and twenty thousand.'

We suppose too that the incident in 1 Chronicles 5:18–22, where they join with Reuben and Manasseh against the Hagarites and Jetur and Nephish and Nodab, is but one of a hundred similar expeditions.[85] Out go the troops, all of them 'sons of valour', with buckler, sword and bow, and dash upon the foe. But for a time the Hagarites and their allies 'troop upon them' bravely, till 'they cry to God in the battle, and he is entreated of them; because they put their trust in him'. Then Gad and his allies 'troop upon the heel' of the fleeing foe, taking 100,000 captives and immense booty. Nor is it unworthy of notice, that in these instances Gad comes on the field to help others, as his father may be said to have done when Leah cried, 'A troop cometh!' The same characteristic will again appear in what is said of him in the blessing of Moses (Deuteronomy 33:20–21).[86]

The Lord directed that Gad should receive a broad territory, the conquered kingdom of Sihon, where he might have ample room for development eastward, when his warlike propensities should impel him. To this, 'blessed be he that enlargeth

---

[85] 'The sons of Reuben, and the Gadites, and half the tribe of Manasseh, of valiant men, men able to bear buckler and sword, and to shoot with bow, and skilful in war, were four and forty thousand seven hundred and threescore, that went out to the war. And they made war with the Hagarites, with Jetur, and Nephish, and Nodab. And they were helped against them, and the Hagarites were delivered into their hand, and all that were with them: for they cried to God in the battle, and he was intreated of them; because they put their trust in him. And they took away their cattle; of their camels fifty thousand, and of sheep two hundred and fifty thousand, and of asses two thousand, and of men an hundred thousand. For there fell down many slain, because the war was of God. And they dwelt in their steads until the captivity.'

[86] 'And of Gad he said, Blessed be he that enlargeth Gad: he dwelleth as a lion, and teareth the arm with the crown of the head. And he provided the first part for himself, because there, in a portion of the lawgiver, was he seated; and he came with the heads of the people, he executed the justice of the LORD, and his judgments with Israel.'

Gad' has reference, while Gad is described as a 'lion' or 'lion-ess, lying down', after tearing 'the arm lifted up to defend the crown of the head'.[87]

Then it is added, 'And he looked out for himself the first fruit,' for he got his settlement among the very first of the tribes, thus acquiring what might be called 'the first fruit portion'. Yet there was no selfishness in this settlement, and therefore 'blessed be he that gave him that ample portion'.

'For, though ensconced, there, in a territory assigned him by the Lawgiver, he came (to join) the heads of the people; in fel-lowship with Israel, to execute the justice of the Lord, and his judgments' (Deuteronomy 33:21).[88] The reference here is to the memorable fact that Gad, along with Reuben and half-Manasseh, passed over Jordan with the other tribes, and took part with them in all their wars with the Canaanites. In this, Gad seems to have taken the lead very characteristically, for is it not as at his father's birth, 'a troop cometh' to aid in clearing the field and securing triumph?

Jephthah was of this tribe, and in his own person certainly it might be said again, 'A troop cometh,' when he so trium-phantly drove out the Ammonites, overcoming those who had overcome so long.[89] Jephthah was a man of Gilead, and Gilead belonged to Gad.

---

[87] Deuteronomy 33:20. 'And of Gad he said, Blessed be he that enlargeth Gad: he dwelleth as a lion, and teareth the arm with the crown of the head.'
[88] KJV: '... because there, in a portion of the lawgiver, was he seated; and he came with the heads of the people, he executed the justice of the LORD, and his judgments with Israel.'
[89] Judges 11:32. 'So Jephthah passed over unto the children of Ammon to fight against them; and the LORD delivered them into his hands.'

To Gad also belonged several places associated with remarkable events—Jabesh-Gilead, Ramoth-Gilead, Peniel, Mahanaim—but none more renowned than Mount Gilead, the hill of balsam trees,[90] the spot where Jacob and Laban made their covenant (perhaps under the shade of one of these groves), calling the spot Galeed, the 'heap of witness'. It still has traces of its former romantic beauty, but no one ever finds the balsam tree. It has disappeared from Gilead, as it has from the valley of Jericho.

This tribe, warlike as it was, no sooner joined in the idolatries of Israel than it felt itself powerless against Jehovah's anger. It was one of the first portions of Israel's land that fell under the power of Tiglath-pileser, who eventually carried away the inhabitants into captivity. The modern Nestorians are in part descended from Gad, for comparing 2 Kings 15:29 with 1 Chronicles 5:26,[91] we find the region of Gilead was carried to the far-off mountains and rivers of Media and Persia, there described. Yes, Gilead, the very heart of Gad, was torn out of him and left to the mercy of strangers, because Jehovah had been forsaken and his covenant grace rejected.

> Bless'd tribe of Gad, when Israel's sick,
> sought by physician's skill,
> and found the balm which healed their wounds
> on fragrant Gilead-hill.

---

[90] An allusion to the balm of Gilead. [Editor]

[91] 2 Kings 15:29: 'In the days of Pekah king of Israel came Tiglath-pileser king of Assyria, and took Ijon, and Abel-beth-maachah, and Janoah, and Kedesh, and Hazor, and Gilead, and Galilee, all the land of Naphtali, and carried them captive to Assyria.' 1 Chronicles 5:26: 'And the God of Israel stirred up the spirit of Pul king of Assyria, and the spirit of Tilgath-pilneser king of Assyria, and he carried them away, even the Reubenites, and the Gadites, and the half tribe of Manasseh, and brought them unto Halah, and Habor, and Hara, and to the river Gozan, unto this day.'

Troops of disease assailed thee then;
to scale thy heights they passed;
but Gilead's balm gave health to all.
'Gad overcame at last.'

Now all in vain seek we for cure,
O Gilead, on thy brow;
for him whose grace was Gilead's balm
thy nation hateth now.

Not even the types of health and joy
within thy land remain;
the thorn and thistle have o'erspread
the mountain and the plain.

Messiah, he is Gilead's balm,
he poured for man his blood.
O tribes of Israel, welcome him,
welcome the Christ of God.

Long have thy foes, troop upon troop,
their chains around thee cast;
but welcome him, and thou art free!
'Gad overcomes at last.'

ANONYMOUS

8 Asher

IT is a peculiarity of Hebrew names that they almost always express the feelings or refer to the circumstances of the parent at the time of the child's birth. In Leah's case there was a good deal that spoke of her dependence on the Lord in the earlier part of her family life; there is little of this looking up to God to be found afterwards. Her handmaid Zilpah bears another son, and Leah expresses her joy (Genesis 30:12–13),[92] exclaiming, 'This is among my happy things,' or, 'Happy am I, for the daughters will congratulate me on my good fortune.'[93] And thus it was that this son got the name Asher, 'the happy one'.

His blessing in Genesis 49:20 corresponds with his name at birth, still speaking of felicity: 'Out of Asher cometh fatness as his bread, and he giveth royal dainties.'[94]

He received a very fruitful soil for his lot—the lowlands of Carmel, abounding in olive oil and wheat, 'bread and fatness'. Some think that it was Asher's territory that furnished the twenty thousand measures of wheat that were sent to Hiram

---

[92] 'And Zilpah Leah's maid bare Jacob a second son. And Leah said, Happy am I, for the daughters will call me blessed: and she called his name Asher.'

[93] KJV: 'And Leah said, Happy am I, for the daughters will call me blessed.'

[94] KJV: 'Out of Asher his bread shall be fat, and he shall yield royal dainties.'

by Solomon (1 Kings 5:11).[95] His vicinity [proximity] to Tyre and Zidon enabled him to bring in royal luxuries ('a king's delights') from these princely cities, and to distribute them among the tribes; this may be meant by his 'giving'.

His territory was a narrow strip of land comparatively, but all the more remarkable is its abundance, tempting his people to indolent enjoyment, as Deborah complained in her song: 'Asher continued on the seashore, and abode in his creeks' (Judges 5:17).[96]

His happy lot, so far as the produce of the soil went, is again celebrated in the last words of Moses (Deuteronomy 33:24–25): 'Asher is blessed above the sons (*i.e.*, peculiarly blessed among the other sons of Jacob), favoured among his brethren, and he dips his foot in oil.'[97]

The Plain of Acre (or Accho) was his—a plain, the weeds of which at this day are the richest and rankest in all Palestine, and its crops most luxuriant, on account of the moisture of the soil. Thus was he peculiarly favoured. Then oil, emblematic of richness and fatness, is referred to with special appropriateness, because Asher's hills were not clothed with the vines that enriched Judah, but were planted with the olive tree; every slope presenting a grove of vigorous olives to the view of the passer-by. 'Thy shoes (or, thy bolts, or castles) shall be iron and brass, and thy languid rest shall be as thy days.'[98]

---

[95] 'And Solomon gave Hiram twenty thousand measures of wheat for food to his household, and twenty measures of pure oil: thus gave Solomon to Hiram year by year.'

[96] KJV: 'Asher continued on the sea shore, and abode in his breaches.'

[97] KJV: 'And of Asher he said, Let Asher be blessed with children; let him be acceptable to his brethren, and let him dip his foot in oil.'

[98] The Hebrew is word-for-word in agreement with the KJV: 'Thy shoes shall be iron and brass; and as thy days, so shall thy strength

Bolted in, as it were, by his hills—hills that produced iron and copper, and may have at early periods helped to supply Zidon, which Homer calls πολυχαλκος [*polychalkos*—abounding in copper]—this tribe was not to be distinguished in war, but so long as it continued to be a tribe was to be noted only for this plenty of bread.

This 'languid rest' (as the word is generally understood to mean) was to be a feature of Asher to the last, and that it was so very early we have proof in the passage quoted from Deborah's song. It may further be noticed that Asher's 'warrior's shoes' or 'strong-barred fortresses', which seem to signify his mountains, were his protection against the men of Tyre and Zidon (Joshua 19:28–29),[99] who remained unsubdued even in Solomon's days, and must often have threatened to disturb this tribe's repose.

A sort of restful contentedness, we have seen, was a feature of this tribe. Its one noble deed was that mentioned in 1 Chronicles 12:36, when it sent forth its forty thousand warriors, 'expert in war', to the help of David. But they fought no battle, and so it seems to have been with those mentioned in 1 Chronicles 7:40, their prince's 'choice and mighty men of valour', and the twenty-six thousand men 'apt to the war and to battle'.

Some of the names given to those of this tribe are interesting, as we find them in 1 Chronicles 7:30. There is Imnah, 'pros-

---

be.' The Keil and Delitzsch commentary (vol. I, p. 511) expresses the opinion that מִנְעָל (*min'āl*—shoe) is derived from נָעַל (*nā'al*—to bolt), 'a poetical expression for a castle or fortress'. [Editor]

[99] 'And Hebron, and Rehob, and Hammon, and Kanah, even unto great Zidon; and then the coast turneth to Ramah, and to the strong city Tyre; and the coast turneth to Hosah; and the outgoings thereof are at the sea from the coast to Achzib.'

perity' or 'right-handedness', and his sister Serah, 'abundance'. Another female of the tribe (verse 32) bears the name Shua, 'the wealthy one'. And then we have (verse 37) Bezer, 'the golden one'; Hod, 'honour'; Shamma, 'renown'; Ithran, 'eminence'; and the list of names ends with (verse 39) Rezia, 'acceptableness', or 'favour', as if referring to Moses' blessing (Deuteronomy 33:24). In all this there is something very characteristic of Asher, the happy one.

In Moses' blessing, Asher is brought in last, and he exclaims (Deuteronomy 33:29), 'Happy (Asher-like) art thou, O Israel!' There may be here an allusion to the tribe and his peculiar blessing, for in its essence it belongs to all Israel. Indeed, it belongs to the family of God, whether we take his name in itself or the blessings showered down upon him.

The family of God are 'Asher', happy, because of pardon, as Psalm 32:1 sings.[100] They have seen their sins buried in the depths, and 'the daughters of Jerusalem' congratulate them on their felicity. The family of God are 'Asher', happy, because of holiness begun, as sung of in Psalm 119:1;[101] they have entered on the conquest of all their passions, and are getting into the inheritance of holy conformity to God's likeness.

The family of God are 'Asher', happy, amid troubles and trials, for all chastening works for their good, as Psalm 94:12 has sung.[102] Happy are they in death, for the voice from heaven

---

[100] 'Blessed is he whose transgression is forgiven, whose sin is covered.' In this and the following two Psalm citations, the Hebrew word *asher* is translated as 'blessed'. [Hembd]

[101] 'Blessed are the undefiled in the way, who walk in the law of the LORD.'

[102] 'Blessed is the man whom thou chastenest, O LORD, and teachest him out of thy law.'

bids us write on their tomb, 'Happy' (Revelation 14:13),[103] and happy above all at the Lord's coming again, when they shall be greeted with the welcome, 'Happy are they who are called to the marriage supper of the Lamb' (Revelation 19:9).[104]

Oh, true Ashers, eat your royal dainties. Your bread is fatness; you are blessed above angels your brethren. Dip your foot in oil and fear no change, for thy walls and bulwarks are salvation, better than the warrior's shoes or the strongest bars of the mountain fortress, and your rest shall continue endless as eternity. Who would not be an Asherite? Receive God's testimony to his Son; believe as Abraham believed, and all this is yours.

And yet again, we cannot but see in Asher's blessing a sample of what all Israel shall enjoy, undisturbed and unchanging, in the latter days, returning home from all lands. The 'daughters'—men on earth and angels above—shall call them blessed; they shall have their bread and fatness and oil; they shall be blessed above their brethren the Gentile nations, and they shall rest in their lot secure while sun and moon endure.

This shall be yours, O people of Israel, whensoever you, as a nation, welcome him who is Earth's true 'Asher'; whensoever you call him blessed, uttering to him your heart's acceptance, 'Blessed is he that cometh in the name of the Lord' (Matthew 23:39).

* * *

---

[103] 'And I heard a voice from heaven saying unto me, Write, Blessed are the dead which die in the Lord from henceforth.' In the cited texts from Revelation, the Greek word μακάριος [makarios], translated as 'blessed', can also be rendered as 'happy'. [Editor]

[104] KJV: 'Blessed are they which are called unto the marriage supper of the Lamb.'

One has sung of this tribe in the following strain:

> A land of plenty Asher had,
> with olive grove and vineyard clad;
> and God's own promise as his plea
> that 'as his days his strength should be'.
>
> Equipped for warfare Asher was
> with shoes of iron and of brass,
> in God Jehovah's name to smite
> the heaven-defying Amorite.
>
> Enamoured of the fertile soil,
> he dipped his foot in corn and oil;
> to ease he gave his soul a prey,
> in sloth he spent probation's day.
>
> He saw the Canaanite command
> his purple sea, his golden strand;
> nor quenched in blood of haughty Tyre
> pale Ashtaroth and Baal's fire.
>
> And when the voice of Barak's war
> went thundering o'er his rocks afar,
> he sat and listened by his creek,
> through love of ease enthralled and weak.
>
> Supine amid his folds he lay,
> and slept the promised strength away;
> nor ventured on the mighty plea,
> 'And as thy days thy strength shall be.'
>
> For this Assyria's eagle came,
> for this, in land of unknown name,
> his coward sloth and guilty fears
> he mourns with unavailing tears.

But not for aye. From sands and snow
of Orient, pilgrim streams shall flow;
and Jacob's sons shall turn again
to the returning latter rain.

Baal and Ashtaroth no more
shall light their temples on his shore,
when Asher's feet again shall seek
his olive-hills and ancient creek.

Awake, ye slumberers in Zion;
think not that ease is happiness!
But seek the rest of Judah's Lion
when he shall come, the Prince of Peace.

PAULIN

9 Issachar

OUR God is 'the very God of peace' (1 Thessalonians 5:23) and delights to impart his peace. He has 'made peace by the blood of the cross', a peace so full that a sinner may have in his conscience the very counterpart to the satisfaction felt by the Holy One who accepted the out-poured life of the Peacemaker. It is this peace which is offered to us. Its richness and glorious grace are (so to speak) the hire by which God would hire us into the acceptance of it. And then he would have all who find this peace to be peacemakers, proposing to others the peace they have themselves found—in a manner, hiring men into this blessed peace of God by showing them its nature and results. Yes, 'Blessed are the peacemakers' (Matthew 5:9), whether in families, neighbourhoods, or nations, for they shadow forth the Great Peacemaker. But observe, God's peace never leads to sloth or ease. If God speaks peace, his saints do not turn again to folly, whereas man's modes of reaching and maintaining peace do continually result in cherishing inactivity and indolence and self-indulgent ease.

We shall find the history of Issachar presenting these truths to us in some aspects. The story of his birth is as follows (Genesis 30:14–18). As Leah had been alienated from her sister for a time, so also it would seem had Jacob been alienated from her, perhaps on account of her treatment of Rachel. One day young Reuben found in the field some of the pale yellow, strong-smelling mandrakes or love-apples, which to this day in the East are supposed to promote childbearing, and which, at all events, have exhilarating effects. Rachel prevailed on her sister to give up these to her, but the expected effect did not follow, the Lord hereby teaching Rachel the sin of trusting in human devices and natural means.

On the other hand, and to impress this lesson all the more deeply and memorably on Rachel, the Lord at that very time gave to Leah another son, and did this in answer to Leah's prayers, for God hearkened to Leah (verse 17), thus answering Leah's faith while he rebuked Rachel's leaning upon sense [feelings].

Now, it is to be remembered that Leah had acted hitherto in the main with a view of getting back Jacob's affections and producing peace once more in the household. She had her eye upon this when giving Zilpah to Jacob (verse 18) at the expense of her own personal feeling, and with this thought on her mind, she exclaims at the birth of this son, 'God hath given me my hire!' and bestows on him the name Issachar: 'There is reward' or 'Here is hire!' Wages are given her; she sees God in this way owning her efforts.

There was compromise in Leah's dealing. Her giving Zilpah to Jacob was compromise; her giving up the mandrakes on the terms agreed upon was compromise; and the domestic circle enjoyed a calm as the result. In after days, Issachar exhibited in his tribe very much of this peace produced by compromise. Jacob's blessing intimates it with sufficient clearness (Genesis 49:14–15). 'Issachar is a strong ass couching down between two burdens; he saw that rest was good, and the land that it was pleasant, and bowed his shoulder to bear, and became a servant unto tribute.' Delitzsch remarks on this blessing that it says in substance, 'Ease at the cost of liberty will be the characteristic of Issachar.'[105] He shall be like a labourer that is content to work his day's work and get his hire. This tribe

---

[105] Keil and Delitzsch, vol. I, p. 403. [Editor]

shall be like the strong ass, used in carrying burdens, and much employed in agricultural labour: Issachar shall not aim at, or exert himself to attain, political power.

His inheritance, too, shall suit his tastes. While the men of this tribe would rather submit to the yoke than give up ease by struggling in the fight for liberty or renown, their portion of the land presented temptations in this direction. For to Issachar belonged Lower Galilee and the beautiful, fertile, wide, and level plain of Jezreel. In order to preserve the quiet enjoyment of this rich inheritance, he was willing to renounce very much that was nobler. His peace and quiet tended to indolence and inactivity and self-indulgence, all unlike the peace of God.

In the camp this tribe numbered more men than Ephraim (Numbers 1:29–33), but they did no exploits like him. True, we see the 'strong ass' in the mighty array of men fit for war, and the same is seen again when Issachar's princes come forth with Barak and Deborah to battle. His men of valour leave the great plain of Jezreel or Esdraelon (which in part is also the valley of Megiddo). Issachar rises up from 'couching between the burdens' (the 'hurdles' or cattle pens, where the cattle were safely lodged and fed). He leaves his pleasant rest between Tabor and Gilboa, and the hills and plains on every side, with their security and abundance. In that remarkable day, 'Princes in Issachar were with Deborah! And Issachar was like Barak, rushing impetuously into the valley at his feet.' (Judges 5:15).[106]

They showed what the tribe could do, and might always have done, but this very sample of their possible efficiency rendered their inertness and slothful peace at other times more conspicuous. There was one judge from this tribe, Tola

---

[106] KJV: 'And the princes of Issachar were with Deborah; even Issachar, and also Barak: he was sent on foot into the valley.'

(Judges 10:1), eminent, but unwarlike, probably a prudent, quiet ruler. In David's time we read of 87,000 (1 Chronicles 7:5), for there is mention first of 22,600 'valiant men of might' (verse 2), and then (verses 4–5) 'in addition to these were bands of soldiers for war, 36,000 men'.[107] This is surely indicative of the 'strong ass'.

At the same time, however, the other feature appears. 'They had many wives and sons', indicative of self-indulgence. Those who came to David in his adversity are spoken of as men given to thoughtful contemplation, and men who thus got insight into general principles of acting, for they are described as being 'men that had understanding of the times, to know what Israel ought to do' (1 Chronicles 12:32). Of these there were 200 leading men, 'and all their brethren were at their commandment'.

Characteristic enough of the tribe, is it not, to find the 87,000 warriors acquiescing quietly in the sway of what we might call the sages and statesmen of their own race. Tradition says that these men calculated the exact times for the festivals, studying carefully those seasons, and giving 'all their brethren' in Israel the advantage of their study and observation, but 'the times' (עתים—*ethim*) refers to public events, very much in our sense of the expression, as in Psalm 31:15 and 1 Chronicles 29:30.[108] At any rate, they understood God's purpose regarding David, the anointed type of Messiah.

It is interesting to know that that godly Shunammite, who entertained Elisha for the Master's sake, was a woman of Issachar, a woman who, in the best application of Issachar's

---

[107] KJV: 'And with them ... were bands of soldiers for war, six and thirty thousand men.'
[108] Psalm 31:15. 'My times are in thy hand.' 1 Chronicles 29:30. 'With all his reign and his might, and the times that went over him, and over Israel.'

tendency, could say, 'I dwell among my own people' (2 Kings 4:13), refusing to go forth from her quiet fields and home.

We have not yet taken notice of the words of Moses in Deuteronomy 33:18, 'Rejoice ... Issachar, in thy tents.' Moses predicts of him the same general characteristic as Jacob did, for it is the same Spirit who inspires both patriarchs. Moses tells of comfortable rest at home 'in thy tents', and if Issachar seems farther (verse 19) to be joined with Zebulon in the more active employment of 'calling the nations' to the mountain of God, *i.e.*, Jerusalem, still it was in his case chiefly, if not entirely, by attraction, not by aggression. Men of other nations were drawn to his luxuriant valleys, for part of his tribe was 'Lower Galilee', famous for the influx of Gentiles, foreigners who came to trade, and whom the 'men of Issachar, who had understanding of the times' would, no doubt, seek to allure to Jehovah's pure worship, imparting to them the knowledge of the only true God and Saviour.

Reference has been made to its great plains, Jezreel and Megiddo, where oft in times past blood has been poured out by contending armies like water, and where, it may be, armies may again ere long meet for the terrible 'day of Jezreel' and 'battle of Armageddon'. In this sense, Issachar 'bends between two burdens' (Genesis 49:14),[109] for armies have met and will meet each other here, using Issachar's level plains for their own convenience without consulting him.

> Where bloomed in pride of beauty fair Jezreel,
> there Issachar's majestic strength was spread.
> The burden-bearer of the common weal
> he bent between the loads his patient head,
> bearing the Assyrian yoke when Egypt fled,

---

[109] KJV: 'Issachar is a strong ass couching down between two burdens.'

and Egypt's when the Assyrian's curb was broken.[110]
Thy plain was watered oft with blood and tears;
grief for Megiddo's slain is still the token
of future wail, when time's allotted years
have run their chequered course,
and Zion's King appears.

PAULIN

Not only was Jezreel in this tribe: Nain too, where Jesus raised the dead, was here. Nevertheless, peaceful Issachar rejected the Prince of Peace, and has shared to the full in the dispersion and desolation of all Israel, but is permitted to look forward to its close in 'the day of Jezreel' (Hosea 1:11).[111]

Blest be thy portion, Issachar! for One
has trod thy plains who came the world to save.

* * * * * * * * * *

But thou in lands afar a tent and grave
for sins of dark idolatry hast found.
Till taught by heaven to make the better choice,
no home is thine. Yet soon a thrilling sound
thine ear shall hear; a death-awakening voice
shall bid thee once again, 'Within thy tents rejoice.'

* * * * * * * * * *

---

[110] 2 Kings 23:29–30. [Bonar]. 'In his days Pharaoh-nechoh king of Egypt went up against the king of Assyria to the river Euphrates: and king Josiah went against him; and he slew him at Megiddo, when he had seen him. And his servants carried him in a chariot dead from Megiddo, and brought him to Jerusalem, and buried him in his own sepulchre. And the people of the land took Jehoahaz the son of Josiah, and anointed him, and made him king in his father's stead.'
[111] 'Then shall the children of Judah and the children of Israel be gathered together, and appoint themselves one head, and they shall come up out of the land: for great shall be the day of Jezreel.'

Then sighs of deeper grief the air shall fill
than Hadadrimmon's mourning; for the cross
seen in salvation's light all hearts shall thrill.
That sight shall change all glory into dross.
The Prince of Peace proclaims the jubilee!
The day of coming time shall that of Jezreel be.

PAULIN

10 Zebulun

HERE is a general sketch of the lot and history of Zebulun:

While faithful to thy covenant King,
in holy might excelling,
thy haven welcomed storm-tossed ships,[112]
home to thy quiet dwelling.

Thy thousands scattered Jabin's pride,[113]
in Kishon's stormy fight;
thy tens of thousands swept away
the conquering Amorite.

And when the tribes to Salem poured;[114]
their festal tides along,
thy banner on the hill of God
waved with the jubilant song.

O Zebulun, my valleys spread,
fair in the morning's sheen;

---

[112] Genesis 49:13 [Bonar]. 'Zebulun shall dwell at the haven of the sea; and he shall be for an haven of ships; and his border shall be unto Zidon.'
[113] Judges 5:18 [Bonar]. 'Zebulun and Naphtali were a people that jeoparded their lives unto the death in the high places of the field.'
[114] Deuteronomy 33:18 [Bonar]. 'And of Zebulun he said, Rejoice, Zebulun, in thy going out; and, Issachar, in thy tents.'

but fairest when *he* dwelt in thee,[115]
the sinless Nazarene.

Great was thy glory when thou dwell'st
at haven of the sea;
but greatest when *he* sheltered souls
on thy shore, blue Galilee.

And even now in Cana's name,
in Nazareth and its hill,
in Magdala, on Tabor's height,[116]
a fragrance lingers still;

Which yet shall fill the dewy air,
of that long-looked-for day,
when he returns who was thy Light,[117]
returns to shine for aye!'

PAULIN

In Genesis 30:19–20 we read the narrative of Zebulun's birth-time. There was gladness in the tents of Jacob; Leah's voice was heard acknowledging the kindness of the Lord. 'God (he who alone disposes and rules in matters private as well as

---

[115] Matthew 4:13–16 [Bonar]. 'And leaving Nazareth, he came and dwelt in Capernaum, which is upon the sea coast, in the borders of Zabulon and Nephthalim: that it might be fulfilled which was spoken by Esaias the prophet, saying, The land of Zabulon, and the land of Nephthalim, by the way of the sea, beyond Jordan, Galilee of the Gentiles; the people which sat in darkness saw great light; and to them which sat in the region and shadow of death light is sprung up.'
[116] 1 Chronicles 6:77 [Bonar]. 'Unto the rest of the children of Merari were given out of the tribe of Zebulun, Rimmon with her suburbs, Tabor with her suburbs.'
[117] Matthew 4:15–16 [Bonar]. 'The land of Zabulon, and the land of Nephthalim, by the way of the sea, beyond Jordan, Galilee of the Gentiles; the people which sat in darkness saw great light; and to them which sat in the region and shadow of death light is sprung up.'

public) has given me a good dowry,' and she calls it good because of what she anticipated would result from it, *viz.*, 'for now shall my husband dwell with me'.[118]

Writers generally suppose that she used the term זבד [*zabad*] 'to endow' because of its being so far an alliteration with זבל [*zabal*] 'to dwell', playing on the words in the happy moment of her son's birth.[119] She thinks it sure that her bringing so much to her husband (this being her sixth gift to him) will secure his becoming more warmly attached to her, and his ever after dwelling with her. This last of a cluster of gifts will complete her victory over any remaining alienation that may have for a time existed in his mind.

Who does not know that 'a man's gift maketh room for him'? (Proverbs 18:16). 'Whithersoever it turned it prospereth' (Proverbs 17:8). Benefits, kindnesses, gifts, succeed in removing distance, coolness, alienation, when other things have failed. It is so between man and man, and it is even so between God and man—that is, God has used this natural instinct of gratitude for favour as a means of melting down man's enmity. His Spirit raises in our hearts the question, 'What shall I render unto the Lord for all his benefits?'

It is a remarkable clause in Psalm 68:18, 'Thou hast received gifts for men; ... that the LORD God might dwell among them.' View it in two ways. On the one hand, it speaks of gifts induc-

---

[118] 'And Leah conceived again, and bare Jacob the sixth son. And Leah said, God hath endued me with a good dowry; now will my husband dwell with me, because I have born him six sons: and she called his name Zebulun.'

[119] Genesis 30:20. 'And Leah said, God hath endued (זבד—*zabad*) me with a good dowry; now will my husband dwell (זבל—*zabal*) with me because I have born him six sons: and she called his name Zebulun.'

ing the Lord to be a Zebulun to us, to dwell with us, as if persuaded by Christ's gift, Christ's dowry of righteousness, and the glory rendered to the Father's name for us. On the other hand, it speaks of the Lord finding out a way of dwelling with us by leading us to come and dwell with him. He shows us 'the gift of God' and who it is who gives it (John 4:10),[120] thus subduing our resistance, and prevailing over our alienated souls. Was it not thus that (in Zebulun's borders) he prevailed on the 'son of Zebedee' (the name signifies 'dowry') to follow him, holding out the gift, 'I will make you fishers of men'?

Shall we not learn from our God how to allure our fellow men, holding out to them God's great gift of his Son? And so we shall in a higher sense become what Zebulun's tribe became in after days, 'havens to ships', storm-tossed (Genesis 49:13),[121] and callers of others to the mountain, while we show them what God has done (Deuteronomy 33:19).[122]

Jacob's blessing alludes to the meaning of the name 'Zebulun (he whose name signifies dwelling) shall dwell at the haven (or shore) of the seas; he shall be a haven (or shore) for ships; and his border shall be over (על—al) Zidon' (Genesis 49:13).[123]

He is to bring in foreigners to dwell with him by presenting a roadstead for ships—a shore where they may find shelter and anchorage. The Bay of Carmel seems chiefly to be alluded to.

---

[120] 'Jesus answered and said unto her, If thou knewest the gift of God, and who it is that saith to thee, Give me to drink; thou wouldest have asked of him, and he would have given thee living water.'
[121] 'Zebulun shall dwell at the haven of the sea; and he shall be for an haven of ships; and his border shall be unto Zidon.'
[122] 'They shall call the people unto the mountain; there they shall offer sacrifices of righteousness: for they shall suck of the abundance of the seas, and of treasures hid in the sand.'
[123] KJV: '... unto Zidon.'

'Their border went up toward the sea' (Joshua 19:11, compared with 9:1)—that is, the Mediterranean, here called 'the seas', because perhaps of the bay, suggesting a north and a south sea coming in. Others understand 'seas' to refer to the fact that his region stretched from the Mediterranean to the shore of the Sea of Galilee.

But what is meant by 'his border shall be over (עַל—*al*) Zidon'?[124] It intimates that his position would give him easy access to Zidon, and might further suggest that by his ships his border may be said to reach even as far as Zidon. However, the simplest view is that עַל [*al*] is to be understood as 'over', in the sense of superiority—*i.e.*, though he shall never rival Zidon in merchandise and in naval renown, yet his Bay of Carmel shall attract when Zidon fails.

Delitzsch notes that a proof of the genuine antiquity of Jacob's words is furnished by the fact that Zidon, not Tyre, is the city, for Tyre was not then famous—indeed, not founded till the times of the Judges. But renowned as Zidon may have been for luxuries, and even if Zebulun's fisheries, and purple dye found on his shores, and suchlike merchandise should never equal that merchant city, still his tribe has temporal blessings that might allure even Zidon to his borders, besides having the far

---

[124] See in Ugolinus the treatise by Hasæus, *De Zabulonis præ Zidone Præstantiâ* ['The superiority of Zebulun over Zidon']. Thomson (*The Land and the Book*, vol. i, p. 484) supposes that Zidon may have then been equivalent to Phœnicia; and understands 'his border shall reach unto Zidon' to signify that Zebulun's boundaries should stretch towards Phœnicia. [Bonar]
Blaisius Ugolinus (the latinized form of Blasio Ugolino) was an eighteenth-century Italian polymath, best known for writing a large collection of treatises on Jewish antiquities. Due to his familiarity with Talmudic literature, it has been surmised that he was a Jewish convert. [Editor]

greater blessings referred to by Moses in Deuteronomy 33:19 and spoken of clearly by Isaiah (9:1–2).[125]

Moses, in his blessing, alludes to one of the characteristics of this tribe, his attractive influence, when he joins him with Issachar in the prediction (Deuteronomy 33:19): 'They shall call nations to the mountain; there they offer sacrifice of righteousness.'

That the Gentiles were allured to dwell with Zebulun we know well, for 'Galilee of the Gentiles' was in part his territory. But Moses seems to say that while these nations were attracted by them to the mountain where sacrifice should be offered, it was in the first instance by Zebulun's produce and merchandise that they were drawn: 'For they shall seek the abundance of the seas, and the hidden treasures of the sand'[126]—earthly good things—fish, purple shells, glass, and all besides that their position on 'the seas' enabled them to traffic [trade] in. In spite, too, of Delitzsch's remark to the contrary, 'Rejoice, Zebulun, in thy going out' (Deuteronomy 33:18) is a clause that does seem to refer to this tribe's enterprise and traffic [trade], although we have no record of their undertakings in this department.

But Zebulun was at all times ready not only to draw others in to dwell with him, but 'to go out' when occasion required. His numbers stood high in the enumeration in the wilderness: first 57,000 and then 60,000 fighting men. When Barak and Deborah summoned Israel to battle, Zebulun came at once.

---

[125] 'Nevertheless the dimness shall not be such as was in her vexation, when at the first he lightly afflicted the land of Zebulun and the land of Naphtali, and afterward did more grievously afflict her by the way of the sea, beyond Jordan, in Galilee of the nations. The people that walked in darkness have seen a great light: they that dwell in the land of the shadow of death, upon them hath the light shined.'
[126] KJV: 'For they shall suck of the abundance of the seas, and of treasures hid in the sand.'

'Take with thee', said Deborah to Barak, 'ten thousand men of the children of Naphtali, and of the children of Zebulun' (Judges 4:6), and her song celebrates them as 'a people that jeoparded their lives unto the death in the high places of the field' (Judges 5:18).

In Gideon's day, they are among those who 'came up to meet him' when he blew the trumpet, and sent his messengers (Judges 6:35).[127] Nor were they wanting in the day of David's trial and distress, for 50,000 of them came to help God's anointed king in his adversity—men that 'went forth to battle' (1 Chronicles 12:33): יוצאי [yotsei—going forth], compared with צדק [tsedeq—righteousness] (Deuteronomy 33:19). 'Expert in war, with all instruments of war, fifty thousand that could keep rank, they were not of double heart.'[128]

The men of this tribe in the days of Hezekiah, if they are not found calling others to the mountain where sacrifice was offered, at any rate encouraged others to go by sending many of their number up to Jerusalem to keep the Passover. 'Divers of Zebulun humbled themselves, and came to Jerusalem' (2 Chronicles 30:11). 'A multitude of the people, many of Issachar and Zebulun' (2 Chronicles 30:18).

Some understand that Ibzan the judge, mentioned in Judges 12:8,[129] was of this tribe, and the Bethlehem where he was buried is, in that case, the city mentioned in Joshua 19:15, the name and remains of which have been found by travellers in

---

[127] 'And he sent messengers throughout all Manasseh; who also was gathered after him: and he sent messengers unto Asher, and unto Zebulun, and unto Naphtali; and they came up to meet them.'
[128] KJV: 'Of Zebulun, such as went forth to battle, expert in war, with all instruments of war, fifty thousand, which could keep rank: they were not of double heart.'
[129] 'And after him [Jephthah] Ibzan of Bethlehem judged Israel.'

the midst of an oak forest.[130] But at any rate, Elon (Judges 12:11–12) was of this tribe, for with curious emphasis it is repeated, 'Elon, a Zebulonite, judged Israel ten years. ... Elon, the Zebulonite died, and was buried in Aijalon, in the country of Zebulun.'

And one other fact let us not fail to remember, namely, Nazareth was in this tribe. The tribe, whose name means 'dwelling', was the tribe in whose bounds the incarnate Son of God dwelt thirty years, and on the shore of one of its seas how often was he to be found? If nought else had distinguished Zebulun, this alone would have been enough in our eyes to fill up the prediction: 'His border shall be above Zidon.'

Rejoice, Zebulun, and call the nations to the mountain where sacrifices of righteousness are offered. Invite all men hither, for in God manifest in the flesh—Jesus of Nazareth—they shall find better than all earthly wealth, better than the abundance of the seas. They shall find the one great sacrifice which supersedes all others; they shall discover that the Word made flesh, who dwelt among us, is the best of hidden treasures, and shall agree with us that his presence has made the border of Zebulun far to excel the border of Zidon.

---

[130] Joshua 19:15–16. 'And Kattath, and Nahallal, and Shimron, and Idalah, and Bethlehem: twelve cities with their villages. This is the inheritance of the children of Zebulun according to their families, these cities with their villages.'

11 Joseph (Ephraim and Manasseh)

RACHEL loved the Lord, and acknowledged him in her domestic life. But she had something of the fretfulness of Jonah, peevishly finding 'good cause to be angry' because the Lord had shut up her womb. On this very account, the Lord, chastising her as a daughter, long withheld her desire.

She on her part ceased not to cry to the Lord, and perhaps was stirred to more importunate pleading by Leah having recently called her daughter Dinah ('the judgment-one'), as if in triumph over Dan ['judging']. At all events, she did call on the Lord, and 'God remembered Rachel' (Genesis 30:22) and opened her womb. No sooner was her son born than she gave glory to God. 'God (Elohim) has taken away my reproach; Jehovah will add to me another son,' calling his name Joseph,[131] which has a peculiar combination of allusions in itself. The verse has 'Jehovah' in it; it has אסף [*asaf* or *Asaph*] 'take away' in it; and it has יסף [*yasaf*] 'add' in it; so that יוסף [*Yosef* or *Joseph*] is really 'he by whom Jehovah takes away reproach, and by whom he gives a pledge of his readiness to give more'.

---

[131] Genesis 30:23–24. 'And she conceived, and bare a son; and said, God hath taken away my reproach: and she called his name Joseph; and said, The LORD shall add to me another son.' See page 56, (footnote 65) for the differentiation of Elohim and Jehovah. [Editor]

There is something noble in Rachel's thoughts on this occasion; she adores God in his liberality and willingness to bless. Once let him begin, and he will go on, for if the hindrance is removed, he delights to give. The floodgates once opened, the water pours along. Is it not so in salvation? Has he found his way to us, bestowing 'repentance and remission of sins'? Then the way is open for more, and he will give daily mercy, increasing holiness, abounding peace, endless glory. Indeed, Rachel's language, 'The Lord will add', is substantially Paul's: 'Now to him that is able (signifying heart as well as hand) to do exceeding abundantly above all we ask or think' (Ephesians 3:20).

It has been remarked by writers that the birth of a son by a mother who was long childless is, in Scripture, always referred to as a special boon of rare kindness, and that such a son is given to carry out some peculiar designs. At all events, God's dealing with Rachel was rightly interpreted by her, and her acknowledgment of divine liberality met with divine approval. Her son Joseph's tribe became a most notable illustration of the Lord's bounteous giving 'good measure, pressed down, and shaken together, and running over' (Luke 6:38).

Rachel magnified the Lord's liberality, as we have said. She opened her mouth wide, and the Lord filled it. Might we not get her ample measure of blessing were we, like her, putting unbounded confidence in his giving heart? The Lord did show himself in her son's history, far more fully than in her own, as the God who 'takes away reproach', and who goes on 'adding' to former favours.

Hear Jacob's blessing (Genesis 49:22–26). 'A fruitful bough is Joseph, a fruitful bough by a well, whose branches run over the wall' (verse 22).[132] You call to mind Joseph's wondrous

---

[132] KJV: 'Joseph is a fruitful bough, even a fruitful bough by a well; whose branches run over the wall.'

greatness in Egypt, how his power was felt and his kindly shadow in every corner of the land, as well as in Goshen. Next, you call to mind his two sons, Ephraim and Manasseh, how they increased in their descendants till they formed two great tribes, 'his branches running over the wall', for no other of Jacob's sons multiplied in this manner. You call to mind how Manasseh's territory was on either side Jordan, Joseph's branches 'running over the wall' here again—not to speak of his many mighty ones, and his noble bands, with such men as Joshua, excelling in true fruitfulness, in the forefront.

But we read on (verses 23–24): 'The archers sorely grieved him, shot at him, and hated him: but his bow abode in strength, and the arms of his hands were made strong by the hands of Jacob's Mighty One.' [133] His reproach was turned away and recoiled on his foes, and all this was done by Jehovah; it came 'from thence, from the Shepherd, the stone of Israel; from the God of thy father, who shall help thee; from the Almighty who shall bless thee.' [134] Yes, from him of whom thy mother said, 'He shall add.'

He shall ever be found true to his character, going on 'helping' and going on 'blessing'. And what a flood of blessing! 'Blessings of heaven above'—the rain and dew dropping on his territory plenteously. 'Blessings of the deep that lieth beneath'—fountains and rivers pouring out their gushing floods. 'Blessings of the breast and of the womb'—increase of every kind in full measure. [135]

---

[133] KJV: 'The archers have sorely grieved him, and shot at him, and hated him: but his bow abode in strength, and the arms of his hands were made strong by the hands of the mighty God of Jacob.'
[134] KJV, verses 24–25: '... (from thence is the shepherd, the stone of Israel): even by the God of thy father, who shall help thee; and by the Almighty, who shall bless thee.'
[135] KJV, verse 25: 'Blessings of heaven above, blessings of the deep that lieth under, blessings of the breasts, and of the womb.'

The giving or 'adding' bounty of Jehovah towards Joseph is so full, so singularly full, that Jacob exclaims, with allusion to the more general and indefinite blessing, common to all the tribes, pronounced by Isaac as well as declared to Abraham: 'Thy father's blessings rise high (like the Flood's waters) above my progenitors' blessings; up to the everlasting hills. Let them be on Joseph's head! On the crown of the head of him who is distinguished among his brethren.'[136]

The surpassing richness of his territory, even to the summit of its hills (witness the hills of Samaria, Bashan, and Gilead!) with the accompanying abundance of all things, and the population revelling in this luxuriance: this, and much more, is included in this blessing on him who was 'separated', in the sense of being above the rest in dignity and influence.

But shall we be able to trace in Moses' blessing (Deuteronomy 33:13–17)[137] any recognition of Rachel's God, who shows in Joseph's case that he will honour them who hesitate not to expect that he will give, and give again? It is even so: Moses does discern in Joseph's lot the same exuberant bounty of

---

[136] KJV, verse 26: 'The blessings of thy father have prevailed above the blessings of my progenitors unto the utmost bound of the everlasting hills: they shall be on the head of Joseph, and on the crown of the head of him that was separate from his brethren.'

[137] 'And of Joseph he said, Blessed of the LORD be his land, for the precious things of heaven, for the dew, and for the deep that coucheth beneath, and for the precious fruits brought forth by the sun, and for the precious things put forth by the moon, and for the chief things of the ancient mountains, and for the precious things of the lasting hills, and for the precious things of the earth and fulness thereof, and for the good will of him that dwelt in the bush: let the blessing come upon the head of Joseph, and upon the top of the head of him that was separated from his brethren. His glory is like the firstling of his bullock, and his horns are like the horns of unicorns: with them he shall push the people together to the ends of the earth: and they are the ten thousands of Ephraim, and they are the thousands of Manasseh.'

Jehovah. We need not quote the words in full, but there are a few things specified which illustrate the history of Joseph's double tribe.

He sings of the accomplishment of Jacob's blessing in the gift of copious, overflowing, plenteous waters; and the precious productions ripened by the 'sun and moon', and given to Joseph at the regular periods in succession, so that his very hills—with their olives, vines, metals, pastures, spices—contributed to form a sample of 'earth and its fulness', and all through the 'goodwill of him who dwelt in the bush', *i.e.*, the free sovereign favour of Jehovah who at the bush intimated how he meant to dwell with undeserving men, blessing and not consuming them.

But Moses proceeds to tell some distinctive features of Joseph's tribe—namely, in regard to its double nature: 'The firstborn of his bullock, glory is to him; even buffalo horns are his horns.'[138] This is Ephraim, whom Jacob raised to the position of firstborn (Genesis 48:8).[139] Ephraim was to have special honour: he was, in Joshua, to push the nations of Canaan, and in after days to seat himself on the throne of the Ten Tribes.[140]

---

[138] Bonar follows the interpretation given in Keil and Delitzsch, vol. I, p. 506, where the word translated as 'unicorn' in the KJV (and other Protestant versions) is rendered as 'buffalo'. [Editor]

[139] KJV: 'And Israel beheld Joseph's sons, and said, Who are these?' See verses 13 and 14: 'And Joseph took them both, Ephraim in his right hand toward Israel's left hand, and Manasseh in his left hand toward Israel's right hand, and brought them near unto him. And Israel stretched out his right hand, and laid it upon Ephraim's head, who was the younger, and his left hand upon Manasseh's head, guiding his hands wittingly; for Manasseh was the firstborn.'

[140] In the symbolical sealing, Revelation 7:8, Joseph evidently stands for Ephraim, for verse 6 has Manasses separately. [Bonar]

But at the same time, it is not only in Ephraim, 'the mighty tribe', that Joseph is to be represented: in this instance one son of Jacob is to originate two tribes. 'And they' (these sons of Joseph whom you see) 'are the myriads of Ephraim! And they are the thousands of Manasseh!'[141]

Who does not feel that the horn of plenty has been emptied on this tribe?

> Blest of the Lord was Joseph's land
> with sacred treasure of the dew and deep;
> blest by the moon in Nature's hour of sleep,
> and by the sun with autumn's golden heap,
> to fill the Reaper's hand.
>
> His was the strength of ancient hills,
> the treasure of the pasture and the mine;
> and, crowning all, a blessing more divine,
> clear in that light that made the bush to shine,
> leapt his rejoicing rills.
>
> Blest was his portion when beside
> the well of Sychar sat the Holy One,
> footsore and weary 'neath a shadeless sun,
> opening to one who sin's career had run
> salvation's healing tide.
>
> Bald Ebal and fair Gerizim,
> ages have passed, but lightly o'er your brow;
> but o'er your wandering tribes hangs even now
> the curse that hath avenged the broken vow
> of faithless Ephraim.

---

[141] KJV, verse 17: 'And they are the ten thousands of Ephraim, and they are the thousands of Manasseh.'

Yet to his record's promise true,
the Man of Sychar cometh once again,
all Gerizim's rich blessings in his train,
to pour on Joseph's land the latter rain,
and Shiloh's life renew.

PAULIN

It would not be possible, within our limits, to sketch with any fulness the history of the teeming thousands and ten thousands of Joseph. We might speak of Ephraim's cities—Shiloh, Sychem, Tirzah, Samaria—and of Manasseh's inheritance on the west of Jordan, stretching from Beth-shan to where afterwards rose Caesarea; and then of his portion in the east, where stood the sixty cities called Havoth-jair, where the hill of Bashan reared its head, with a plain at its foot extending in one unbroken expanse, flat as the surface of a lake, for fifty miles. Truly Joseph's spreading branches 'ran over the wall'.

We may, however, glean a few less-known facts about these sons of Joseph from the book of Chronicles. It is recorded that 'there fell some of Manasseh to David, as he went to Ziklag, Adnah, and Jozabad, and Jediael, and Michael, and Jozabad, and Elihu, and Zilthai, captains of the thousands that were of Manasseh' (1 Chronicles 12:20). These seven leaders and their men took the part of the despised and persecuted son of Jesse, casting in their lot with him in the day of his calamity. 'And they helped David against the band of the rovers (the roving Amalekites and others): for they were all mighty men of valour, and were princes[142] in the host.'

In verse 31 it is said that they numbered eighteen thousand men. This was on the west side of Jordan, but their brethren on the east side also came: 'of the half tribe of Manasseh, on the other side of Jordan', along with a company of Reubenites

---

[142] KJV: 'captains'.

and Gadites,[143] reminding us of the early days when these allied tribes crossed over to the help of Joshua. They came 'with all manner of instruments of war for the battle, an hundred and twenty thousand'. Very deep hold had the cause of David taken on their hearts, and David's cause was the cause of God, so that we may say there was in those days no common interest felt for the things of God in Joseph's borders. It was most honourable to them, and is a noble example to us, for in this there is a type. As they adhered to David, the anointed, in his day of adversity, so are we to follow the true David in days of evil, such as the present times are, for 'if we suffer with him, we shall also reign with him'.

We should have noted that Ephraim also sent to the same cause his 'twenty thousand and eight hundred' (verse 30), 'mighty men of valour, famous throughout the house of their fathers'. Well did it become the descendants of him who is described as shot at by the archers, sorely grieved, and hated (Genesis 49:23), thus to come forward and take the part of God's servant in days when the archers shot at him, as he sang in Psalm 64:3–4.[144]

From another part of 1 Chronicles, we glean something more. In chapter 7:15 we find Machir of Manasseh marrying Maachah of Benjamin, thus again illustrating Joseph's branches 'running over the wall'. In verse 16 it is told that this Maachah called her firstborn Peresh, as if alluding to this spreading of Joseph's vine, for Peresh signifies 'spreading'.

---

[143] 1 Chronicles 12:37: 'And on the other side of Jordan, of the Reubenites, and the Gadites, and of the half tribe of Manasseh, with all manner of instruments of war for the battle, an hundred and twenty thousand.'
[144] '... who whet their tongue like a sword, and bend their bows to shoot their arrows, even bitter words: that they may shoot in secret at the perfect: suddenly do they shoot at him, and fear not.'

But we gather more regarding Ephraim. In that same chapter, verses 21–23,[145] we find that he to whom the blessings of Jacob and of Moses held up such bright visions of prosperity was at first the most vexed and tried of all Jacob's sons, even like his father Joseph, and Joseph's mother, Rachel. For after he had called one son Zabad, 'dowry'; another Shuthelah, 'plantation of greenness'; another Ezer, 'help'; and another Elead, 'God adorns', his prospects were suddenly and sorely darkened. The men of Gath (native Hittites, it may be, before the time of the later Philistines) in some engagement slew these promising sons of Ephraim! It is thought that these sons of Ephraim had gone out of Goshen and entered Palestine, and assailed these men of Gath, perhaps thinking that God would at that time give the people into their hands, pushing them before them, since the land was theirs by promise. But, as afterwards in the siege of Ai, the Lord taught that it is not a good cause itself that gives victory, but the actual and present help of him whose cause it is.

Ephraim mourned bitterly and long, perhaps alarmed as well as amazed, for it seemed as if Jehovah's words were falling to the ground. He called his infant, then born, Beriah, 'one born in misfortune'.

But the clouds soon broke. His daughter Sherah (1 Chronicles 7:24) is found on the highlands of Palestine, near where her brothers perished, and becomes renowned, building the two towns of Beth-horon the nether and the upper—a woman, the founder of Ephraim's greatness, as if a foreshadowing of the

---

[145] 'And Zabad his son, and Shuthelah his son, and Ezer, and Elead, whom the men of Gath that were born in that land slew, because they came down to take away their cattle. And Ephraim their father mourned many days, and his brethren came to comfort him. And when he went in to his wife, she conceived, and bare a son, and he called his name Beriah, because it went evil with his house.'

time when the Virgin should bring to earth its true ray of hope!

There flowed also, ere long, a full stream from Beriah's fountain, beginning in Rephah and Reseph, 'riches', and 'flame of lightning', till it reached Nun and Joshua (1 Chronicles 7:25–27).[146]

It was thus that the Lord tried faith before he honoured it, appearing to extinguish the hopes of Joseph's firstborn ere he brought them to full perfection. Such is the way of our God: the sorrow goes before the joy, even as Messiah is first the Man of Sorrows, and then crowned with glory and honour.

Nor has Joseph been finally given over. His blessing is in reversion, for Jeremiah says (Jeremiah 31:5, 12, 14) of 'Ephraim, the Lord's firstborn' (verses 9, 20), 'Thou shalt yet plant vines upon the mountain of Samaria; the planters shall plant, and shall eat them as common things, for there shall be a day when the watchman upon Mount Ephraim shall cry, Arise, and let us go up to Zion, to the LORD our God. ... And they shall come and sing in the height of Zion, and flow together to the goodness of the LORD, for wheat, and for wine, and for oil, for the sons of the flock and of the herd; and their soul shall be like a well-watered garden,[147] and they shall not sorrow any more at all. ... And I will satiate the soul of the priests with fatness, and my people shall be satisfied with my goodness.' Surely this is the very God of Joseph!

---

[146] 'And Rephah was his son, also Resheph, and Telah his son, and Tahan his son, Laadan his son, Ammihud his son, Elishama his son, Non [Nun] his son, Iehoshua [Joshua] his son.'
[147] KJV: '... and their soul shall be as a watered garden'.

12 Benjamin

THE only one of the twelve patriarchs born in Palestine was Benjamin. The circumstances of his birth are well known (Genesis 35:16–20).[148] His mother Rachel, after an interval of nearly twenty years, got this other son from the Lord, but it seems she was feeble and desponding as the hour of birth drew near, and had hard labour. Though her attendant sought to comfort her by saying, 'Fear not, for this also is a son for thee'—words fitted to recall her own faith when her first son was born (chapter 30:24)—she heeded not, but despondingly pronounced 'Ben-oni'—'son of my sorrow'—over the child, and expired.

Tradition still points out the spot where she was buried: every traveller to this day knows 'Rachel's Tomb', midway between Jerusalem and Bethlehem. But Jacob would not perpetuate the sadness, or at least would fain throw over it a gleam of sunshine, and therefore names the child Benjamin, 'son of the

---

[148] 'And they journeyed from Bethel; and there was but a little way to come to Ephrath: and Rachel travailed, and she had hard labour. And it came to pass, when she was in hard labour, that the midwife said unto her, Fear not; thou shalt have this son also. And it came to pass, as her soul was in departing, (for she died) that she called his name Benoni: but his father called him Benjamin. And Rachel died, and was buried in the way to Ephrath, which is Bethlehem. And Jacob set a pillar upon her grave: that is the pillar of Rachel's grave unto this day.'

right hand', expressive of what he hoped for him as well as declaring his strong affection to him for his mother's sake.

Jacob in this did well. He looked at what God might bring out of this calamity, and not simply at the sad event itself. See the patriarch, full of faith, after all the toil and weariness of his long wanderings, and after the bitter anguish caused by Dinah's sin and her brothers' cowardly and atrocious murder of the Sychemites. See the aged saint standing at Rachel's tomb, 'looking not at the things that are seen, but at the things which are not seen', anticipating blessing in the Lord's time and way for this sorest bereavement that had befallen him, and by the name 'Benjamin' sealing his faith.

Rachel looked at affliction on the side of human feeling, and judged by her frame of mind: Jacob viewed it as it can be seen by faith. Nature sees only gloom and cries, 'Ben-oni!' Faith penetrates the gloom and, discovering light beyond, cries 'Benjamin!' Faith is not 'like moonlight on a troubled sea, bright'ning the storm it cannot calm'. [149] Faith calms the waves, for it brings to us him who can say, 'Peace, be still.'

Jacob's blessing on Benjamin (Genesis 49:27) has reference to this scene.[150] Indeed, it is as if his heart were torn up by the memories which the mention of Benjamin called up. But in truth, the future lot of Benjamin and his descendants was to be in keeping with their starting-point: scenes of sorrow passing into scenes of joy.

'Benjamin is a ravening wolf.' He shall be marked by having to do with scenes wherein tearing asunder and violent rending

---

[149] A quotation from *The Loves of the Angels* by Thomas Moore (1779–1852), an Irish poet. [Editor]
[150] 'Benjamin shall ravin as a wolf: in the morning he shall devour the prey, and at night he shall divide the spoil.'

shall be prominent, even as his birth time was a time of rending ties asunder. And yet there shall be to him results of peace
and scenes of triumph. He shall afterwards be like the wolf in
its den, leisurely feasting on its prey after the carnage is over.
'In the morning he shall devour the prey; in the evening divide
the spoil.'

Some of the old Rabbis refer to the fact that Jerusalem and its
altar properly belonged to Benjamin, so that in the sacrifices,
morning by morning, day by day, for about fifteen hundred
years, Benjamin was seen 'ravening like a wolf, devouring the
prey'. If so, we would add, 'In the evening he divided the spoil,'
for if he was Ben-oni in having to do with blood and death,
with victims slain and cut in pieces, with the skin flayed, and
the bones divided, and the fat distributed, yet was he also
Benjamin in having the privilege of seeing by faith the great
sacrifice through these types of the Lamb of God to be slain
for sinners, and afterwards the wondrous honour of actually
having that great sacrifice present in the temple.

Others illustrate Jacob's words by referring to the history of
the deliverance of Israel by Ehud's singular deed of blood, and
to the wolf-like ravening of the tribe in defence of Gibeah
(Judges 20), which was forgotten ere long in the exploits of
Saul, the first king of Israel. They add also the happy times
that at a later period passed over scattered Israel through
Mordecai and Esther, both belonging to this tribe, in whose
case certainly everything at first had the sad aspect of Ben-
oni, but passed completely over to the cheerful sunshine of
Benjamin.

One other fact should not be forgotten. If in the earlier period
of this tribe's history the Ben-oni aspect prevails—'the ravening of the wolf'—yet in Saul's days 'little Benjamin' (Psalm
68:27) became mighty (1 Samuel 9:21, compared with 14:47–

48).[151] And after the days of David you see the Benjamin aspect appear more decidedly still—the dividing of the prey in peace, when this tribe was associated with Judah in holding the sceptre till Shiloh come, returning with Judah from Babylon.

In Ezekiel 48:23 we find him side by side with Judah still, bordering on the holy oblation.[152] Some of the Fathers were convinced that the prophecy went even further in minute fulfilment. They saw in it the history of a notable man of his tribe—Saul of Tarsus—making havoc (ἐλυμάινετο) [elymaineto—havoc] of the Church like a wolf,[153] and dividing the prey with the Church when his heart was turned. Saul becoming Paul the apostle is, in their view, as Ben-oni becoming Benjamin.

The blessing of Moses (Deuteronomy 33:12)[154] gives us the cheerful side, as if he had been led by the inspiring Spirit to dwell as much upon the Benjamin characteristic as Jacob had done on the Ben-oni. Hence he calls him 'beloved of the

---

[151] 1 Samuel 9:21: 'And Saul answered and said, Am not I a Benjamite, of the smallest of the tribes of Israel? and my family the least of all the families of the tribe of Benjamin? wherefore then speakest thou so to me?' 1 Samuel 14:47–48: 'So Saul took the kingdom over Israel, and fought against all his enemies on every side, against Moab, and against the children of Ammon, and against Edom, and against the kings of Zobah, and against the Philistines: and whithersoever he turned himself, he vexed them. And he gathered an host, and smote the Amalekites, and delivered Israel out of the hands of them that spoiled them.'

[152] 'As for the rest of the tribes, from the east side unto the west side, Benjamin shall have a portion.'

[153] 'As for Saul, he made havock of the church, entering into every house, and haling men and women committed them to prison' (Acts 8:3). The Greek word ἐλυμάινετο [elymaineto] comes from λυμαίνομαι [lymainomai]—to defile, make havoc. [Editor]

[154] 'And of Benjamin he said, The beloved of the LORD shall dwell in safety by him; and the LORD shall cover him all the day long, and he shall dwell between his shoulders.'

LORD'—*i.e.*, not beloved of Jacob only, but of the Lord also—a title which is specially appropriate to him as in part possessing that token of God's favour, the temple and part of the holy city within his borders.

The sense of the other clause may be given thus: 'He shall dwell in safety by Jehovah, who shall cover him all the day long.' Jehovah shall be his canopy (חפף [*hofaf*—to cover], compare the חפה [*hupoh*—canopy, defence] of Isaiah 4:5),[155] 'Jehovah shall dwell amid his hills,' especially referring to Jerusalem and his portion of it, though others explain the words, 'Benjamin shall be like a son whom his father carries on his shoulders' (Deuteronomy 33:12, Delitzsch).[156]

O world, the favour of our God changes the lot of sorrow into joy, but your lot, though it is a Benjamin's portion in measure (Genesis 43:34),[157] shall soon become Ben-oni.

It is a singular fact in the history of this tribe that so many of them were left-handed, and yet 'could sling stones at a hair's breadth'. It is singular that so many Benjamins should be left-handed, but specially that this apparent defect and disadvantage should have been remedied by the marvellous skill which distinguished the left-handed ones. This fact is noted of Ehud (Judges 3:15)[158] and of the army of Gibeah, in which

---

[155] 'And the LORD will create upon every dwelling place of mount Zion, and upon her assemblies, a cloud and smoke by day, and the shining of a flaming fire by night: for upon all the glory shall be a defence [חפה—*hupoh*].'

[156] 'Between the shoulders' is equivalent to 'upon the back' (see 1 Samuel 17:6). Keil and Delitzsch, vol. I, p. 503.

[157] 'And he took and sent messes unto them from before him: but Benjamin's mess was five times so much as any of theirs.'

[158] 'But when the children of Israel cried unto the LORD, the LORD raised them up a deliverer, Ehud the son of Gera, a Benjamite, a man

were 'seven hundred chosen men left-handed' (20:16). Was there not something here of Ben-oni turned into Benjamin?

It is not less interesting to find of this tribe mighty men who 'could use *both* the right hand and the left in hurling stones and shooting arrows out of a bow' (1 Chronicles 12:2). These men of might, 'helpers of the war', were of 'Saul's brethren, of Benjamin', so that the dark cloud that lowered on David from the side of Benjamin in the person of Saul is now giving forth bright beams. The names of their leaders are given in full, and then again at verse 16, men of Benjamin joined with men of Judah in going to David, with Amasai at their head. It is still the dark cloud followed by the clear shining after rain.

How honourable and noble these 'brethren of Saul' who, in the day of calamity, discovered God's anointed one and followed him at all hazards! Fit representatives of the true disciples of the Lord now, who forsake kindred and friends to take the side of Christ, suffering with him, that they may in due time reign with him—content to be Ben-onis for a time, that they may for ever be Benjamins.

In 1 Chronicles 8, there is full information given about the descendants of Benjamin on account of their connection with Saul and Jonathan. In the close of that genealogical table appears the infant son of Merib-baal, or Mephibosheth, namely, Micah. In him Jonathan's line was brought very low, almost to extinction, but verses 35 and 36 tell how Micah's family grew and was strong. The first two names in it are Pithon, 'enlargement', and Melech, 'king'. And after a catalogue has been given of illustrious descendants, verse 40 ends

---

lefthanded: and by him the children of Israel sent a present unto Eglon the king of Moab.'

by saying, 'The sons of Ulam were mighty men of valour, archers, and had many sons, and sons' sons, an hundred and fifty. All these are of the sons of Benjamin.'

It is still the same story: the Ben-oni aspect first, and then the 'right hand'. The Lord enlightens the darkness, and in the latter days thus it shall be with this tribe, and with all Israel. Their whole past history might, in some respects, be spoken of as sad and sorrowful, but their future shall be all joy and singing, when the Lord brings back the captivity of his people.

Thy birth-night was a time of love and tears;
thy mother travailed sore.
'Son of my sorrow!' Rachel feebly moaned,
then sank, and all was o'er.

'Son of my right hand,' weeping Jacob cried;
'dearest of sons to me!
That name bear thou; of her who gave thee birth
in endless memory.'

Deep-written in thy tribe's sad history,
one name too oft appears;
from Egypt, Gibeah, and Gilboa's height, [159]
Ben-oni looks in tears.

But when of Israel's revolted tribes
the star in night had died,
'son of the right hand', faithful Benjamin,
still sat at Judah's side.

And though, Ben-oni, ages have swept past,
while thou hast worn the chain,
when evening comes, thou must 'divide the spoil'.
Rise, Benjamin, again!

_____

[159] Genesis 43 and 44; Judges 19 and 20; 1 Samuel 31. [Bonar]

www.ingramcontent.com/pod-product-compliance
Lightning Source LLC
Chambersburg PA
CBHW060120050426
42448CB00010B/1954